Building High-Performance Teams
A Manager's Guide

Kiet Huynh

Table of Contents

Introduction 5
1. Understanding the Importance of High-Performance Teams 5
    1.1 The Impact of Teams on Organizational Success 5
    1.2 Characteristics of High-Performance Teams 7
    1.3 Why High-Performance Teams Matter 10
PART I Preparing for Team Success 13
    2. Assessing Your Team's Current State 13
        2.1 Evaluating Team Performance Metrics 13
        2.2 Identifying Strengths and Weaknesses 16
        2.3 Conducting Team Member Skills Assessment 20
    3. Setting Clear Team Goals and Objectives 23
        3.1 Defining SMART Goals for Your Team 23
        3.2 Aligning Team Goals with Organizational Objectives 27
        3.3 Communicating Goals Effectively to Team Members 31
    4. Establishing Team Norms and Expectations 40
        4.1 Defining Team Norms and Core Values 40
        4.2 Establishing Clear Expectations for Team Members 43
        4.3 Encouraging Accountability and Responsibility 47
PART II Building and Developing Your Team 54
    5. Selecting the Right Team Members 54
        5.1 Identifying Key Competencies and Skills 54
        5.2 Conducting Effective Team Member Recruitment 57
        5.3 Ensuring Diversity and Inclusion in Team Composition 61
    6. Fostering Team Collaboration and Trust 65

TABLE OF CONTENTS

    6.1 Creating a Culture of Open Communication 65

    6.2 Building Trust and Psychological Safety 68

    6.3 Promoting Collaboration and Teamwork 72

7. Providing Effective Team Training and Development 78

    7.1 Assessing Team Training Needs 78

    7.2 Designing Tailored Training Programs 81

    7.3 Implementing Continuous Learning Initiatives 85

PART III Leading and Sustaining High-Performance Teams 91

8. Empowering Team Members through Leadership 91

    8.1 Developing Transformational Leadership Skills 91

    8.2 Empowering Team Members to Make Decisions 94

    8.3 Supporting and Mentoring Team Members 98

9. Managing Team Performance and Feedback 102

    9.1 Setting Clear Performance Expectations 102

    9.2 Providing Constructive Feedback and Recognition 104

    9.3 Addressing Performance Issues Effectively 111

10. Navigating Challenges and Overcoming Obstacles 118

    10.1 Identifying Common Team Challenges 118

    10.2 Implementing Strategies for Overcoming Obstacles 121

    10.3 Building Resilience and Adaptability in Your Team 128

Conclusion 134

    Thank you 136

TABLE OF CONTENTS

PART I: PREPARING FOR TEAM SUCCESS

Introduction

1. Understanding the Importance of High-Performance Teams

1.1 The Impact of Teams on Organizational Success

In the fast-paced and ever-evolving landscape of modern business, the significance of high-performance teams cannot be overstated. These teams serve as the cornerstone of organizational success, wielding immense influence over various facets of operations, productivity, innovation, and ultimately, the bottom line. To comprehend the profound impact of teams on organizational success, it's imperative to delve into the multifaceted dynamics at play.

Driving Innovation and Creativity:

High-performance teams are fertile grounds for fostering innovation and creativity within an organization. By bringing together individuals with diverse backgrounds, skill sets, and perspectives, these teams become incubators for novel ideas and groundbreaking solutions. The synergy generated through collaboration often transcends the sum of individual contributions, leading to breakthrough innovations that propel the organization ahead of competitors. Whether it's devising cutting-edge products, refining processes for efficiency gains, or conceptualizing disruptive strategies, high-performance teams serve as the engine driving innovation within the organizational ecosystem.

Enhancing Productivity and Efficiency:

Efficiency and productivity are the lifeblood of any successful enterprise, and high-performance teams serve as catalysts for optimizing these crucial metrics. Through effective coordination, streamlined communication channels, and a shared commitment to excellence, these teams streamline workflows, eliminate redundancies, and maximize output. By leveraging the strengths of each team member and capitalizing on synergies, high-performance teams achieve remarkable feats with unparalleled efficiency. Whether it's meeting tight deadlines, surpassing production targets, or delivering exceptional customer service, these teams consistently raise the bar for performance across the organization.

Fostering a Culture of Collaboration and Accountability:

At the heart of every high-performance team lies a culture characterized by collaboration, trust, and accountability. Members are not merely individuals working in isolation but integral parts of a cohesive unit with a shared mission and collective goals. By fostering an environment where ideas are freely exchanged, feedback is constructively received, and responsibilities are willingly shouldered, these teams cultivate a sense of ownership and empowerment among members. Each team member understands their role in contributing to the larger objectives of the team and holds themselves accountable for their actions and outcomes. This culture of collaboration and accountability permeates throughout the organization, fostering a positive work environment and driving sustained success.

Adapting to Change and Uncertainty:

In today's volatile business landscape, adaptability is a prerequisite for survival, let alone success. High-performance teams possess the resilience and agility to navigate through periods of change and uncertainty with poise and confidence. Whether it's responding to market disruptions, technological advancements, or unforeseen challenges, these teams exhibit a remarkable ability to pivot swiftly, adjust strategies, and seize emerging opportunities. Through open communication, proactive problem-solving, and a commitment to continuous improvement, high-performance teams not only weather storms but emerge stronger and more resilient, positioning the organization for long-term success.

Building Trust and Cohesion:

Trust is the bedrock upon which high-performance teams are built, and its presence is indispensable for achieving collective goals. Within these teams, trust permeates every interaction, fostering a sense of psychological safety where members feel comfortable taking risks, sharing vulnerabilities, and expressing dissenting opinions. This trust is not forged overnight but cultivated through consistent actions, mutual respect, and transparent communication. As trust deepens, so does the cohesion within the team, enabling seamless collaboration, effective decision-making, and cohesive execution of plans. With trust as their foundation, high-performance teams become unstoppable forces driving organizational success.

In essence, high-performance teams are not just cogs in the organizational machinery but the driving force behind its success. Through their unwavering commitment to excellence, relentless pursuit of innovation, and cohesive collaboration, these teams propel organizations to new heights of achievement. By understanding and harnessing the transformative power of high-performance teams, leaders can unlock the full potential of their workforce and steer their organizations towards sustained growth, resilience, and prosperity.

1.2 Characteristics of High-Performance Teams

High-performance teams are the backbone of successful organizations, driving innovation, productivity, and overall growth. Understanding the key characteristics that define these teams is crucial for managers aiming to cultivate and sustain their performance. In this section, we delve into the essential traits that set high-performance teams apart and explore how fostering these qualities can elevate team effectiveness.

1. Clear Goals and Objectives

High-performance teams are united by a shared sense of purpose and clarity regarding their goals and objectives. Each team member understands their role in achieving these objectives and is committed to contributing their skills and efforts toward their attainment. Clear goals provide direction, alignment, and motivation, guiding team members in prioritizing tasks and making decisions that advance the team's mission.

2. Open Communication and Collaboration

Effective communication lies at the heart of high-performance teams. Members freely exchange ideas, feedback, and information, fostering a culture of transparency, trust, and collaboration. Open communication channels enable rapid problem-solving, innovation, and the sharing of best practices. Team members feel empowered to voice their opinions, knowing that their input is valued and respected, leading to stronger relationships and a deeper sense of belonging within the team.

3. Shared Accountability

High-performance teams operate on the principle of shared accountability, where every member takes ownership of both individual and collective outcomes. Team members hold themselves and each other to high standards of performance, recognizing that their success depends on the collective effort. This shared responsibility cultivates a sense of trust and reliability, as team members strive to fulfill their commitments and support one another in achieving shared objectives.

4. Diversity and Inclusion

Diversity, in terms of backgrounds, perspectives, and skills, is celebrated and embraced within high-performance teams. By bringing together individuals with varied experiences and expertise, teams can tackle complex challenges from multiple angles and generate innovative solutions. Inclusive environments, where every voice is heard and valued, foster creativity, empathy, and a deeper understanding of diverse stakeholders' needs, driving greater organizational success.

5. Adaptive and Resilient

High-performance teams demonstrate agility and resilience in the face of adversity and change. They embrace uncertainty as an opportunity for growth and continuously adapt their strategies and approaches to meet evolving challenges. Team members display flexibility, resourcefulness, and a willingness to learn from both successes and failures, enabling them to navigate turbulent environments with confidence and perseverance.

6. Effective Leadership

Strong leadership is essential for guiding high-performance teams toward success. Effective leaders inspire trust, provide direction, and empower team members to achieve their full potential. They foster a supportive and inclusive culture, set clear expectations, and provide constructive feedback to help individuals and the team as a whole continually improve. By leading by example and serving as champions of the team's vision and values, leaders cultivate a shared sense of purpose and commitment among team members.

7. Continuous Learning and Development

High-performance teams prioritize learning and development as fundamental to their success. They invest in ongoing training, skill-building, and knowledge-sharing initiatives to enhance individual and collective capabilities. By staying abreast of industry trends, best practices, and emerging technologies, team members remain agile and adaptable in a rapidly changing landscape. A culture of continuous learning fosters innovation, creativity, and resilience, positioning the team for sustained excellence over the long term.

8. Results-Oriented

Ultimately, high-performance teams are focused on delivering results and driving meaningful outcomes for the organization. They set ambitious yet achievable targets, track progress against key performance indicators, and celebrate milestones along the way. By prioritizing outcomes over activities and embracing a mindset of continuous improvement, these teams consistently deliver value and make a tangible impact on the organization's success.

In conclusion, high-performance teams exhibit a combination of clear goals, open communication, shared accountability, diversity and inclusion, adaptability, effective leadership, continuous learning, and a results-oriented mindset. By fostering these characteristics, managers can cultivate teams that not only meet but exceed expectations, driving innovation, productivity, and organizational growth.

1.3 Why High-Performance Teams Matter

High-performance teams are the backbone of any successful organization. In today's competitive landscape, where businesses are constantly challenged to innovate, adapt, and deliver results at an unprecedented pace, the importance of high-performance teams cannot be overstated. These teams serve as the driving force behind innovation, productivity, and ultimately, organizational success. In this section, we delve deeper into why high-performance teams matter and explore the myriad ways in which they contribute to the achievement of strategic objectives.

Driving Innovation

Innovation lies at the heart of every successful organization. In today's rapidly evolving business environment, where market dynamics are constantly changing and disruptive technologies are reshaping industries, the ability to innovate is crucial for staying ahead of the curve. High-performance teams play a pivotal role in driving innovation within organizations.

These teams bring together individuals with diverse skill sets, backgrounds, and perspectives, fostering a culture of creativity and collaboration. By leveraging the collective expertise of team members, high-performance teams are able to generate novel ideas, identify emerging opportunities, and develop innovative solutions to complex challenges. Moreover, the dynamic nature of high-performance teams enables them to adapt quickly to changing market conditions, experiment with new approaches, and iterate on ideas until they achieve breakthrough results.

Enhancing Productivity

Productivity is a key determinant of organizational performance. High-performance teams are inherently designed to maximize productivity by optimizing workflows, streamlining processes, and eliminating bottlenecks. These teams are characterized by a strong sense of accountability, clear goals, and effective communication channels, all of which contribute to enhanced efficiency and output.

Furthermore, high-performance teams exhibit a high degree of synergy, where the collective effort of team members exceeds the sum of individual contributions. By leveraging each other's strengths and complementing each other's weaknesses, team members are able to achieve greater results than they could on their own. This synergistic effect not only boosts productivity but also fosters a sense of camaraderie and mutual support among team members, leading to higher levels of engagement and job satisfaction.

Driving Organizational Success

At the end of the day, the ultimate measure of a high-performance team's success is its ability to drive organizational success. High-performance teams are instrumental in achieving strategic objectives, meeting performance targets, and ultimately, gaining a competitive edge in the marketplace.

These teams serve as catalysts for growth, helping organizations expand into new markets, launch innovative products, and capitalize on emerging trends. Moreover, high-performance teams act as ambassadors for organizational culture, embodying core values such as excellence, integrity, and collaboration. By consistently delivering exceptional results and setting the bar high for performance, these teams inspire others within the organization to strive for excellence and contribute to the collective success.

In conclusion, high-performance teams are not just a nice-to-have; they are a strategic imperative for organizations looking to thrive in today's fast-paced and competitive business landscape. By driving innovation, enhancing productivity, and driving organizational success, these teams serve as the engine of growth and prosperity, propelling organizations to new heights of achievement.

PART I
Preparing for Team Success

2. Assessing Your Team's Current State

2.1 Evaluating Team Performance Metrics

Evaluating team performance metrics is a critical aspect of understanding the current state of your team. These metrics provide valuable insights into how effectively your team is functioning, where improvements can be made, and what strengths can be leveraged. In this section, we will explore the various types of performance metrics that managers can use to assess their teams.

Key Performance Indicators (KPIs)

Key Performance Indicators, or KPIs, are specific metrics that are directly tied to the objectives and goals of the team. These metrics help managers gauge the overall performance and effectiveness of the team in achieving its objectives. KPIs can vary depending on the nature of the team and its goals, but common examples include:

- *Revenue Generated:* For sales teams, revenue generated is a crucial KPI that directly reflects the team's success in closing deals and driving business.

- *Customer Satisfaction Score (CSAT):* Customer-facing teams often use CSAT as a KPI to measure how satisfied customers are with the products or services provided.

- *Productivity:* Productivity metrics such as output per hour or tasks completed can be valuable for assessing the efficiency of operational teams.

It's essential to select KPIs that align with the overarching goals of the team and provide meaningful insights into performance.

Quality Metrics

In addition to quantity-based metrics like productivity or revenue, quality metrics offer insights into the effectiveness and excellence of the team's outputs. These metrics focus on aspects such as accuracy, reliability, and customer satisfaction. Some common quality metrics include:

- *Error Rate:* For teams involved in data entry, manufacturing, or software development, tracking the error rate can help identify areas for improvement in accuracy and quality.

- *Customer Complaints:* Monitoring the number and nature of customer complaints can highlight potential issues with product or service quality.

- *Defect Rate:* In manufacturing or production environments, tracking the defect rate provides insights into the quality of the output and helps identify areas for process improvement.

By assessing both quantity and quality metrics, managers can gain a comprehensive understanding of their team's performance and identify areas for optimization.

Team Dynamics Metrics

Team dynamics metrics focus on the interpersonal relationships, communication patterns, and collaboration within the team. These metrics are essential for assessing the overall health and cohesion of the team. Some examples of team dynamics metrics include:

- *Employee Engagement:* Surveys or assessments measuring employee engagement can provide insights into the team's morale, motivation, and commitment to the organization.

- *Communication Effectiveness:* Analyzing communication patterns, such as frequency of interactions, response times, and clarity of messages, can help identify communication bottlenecks or issues.

- *Team Cohesion:* Assessing factors such as trust among team members, willingness to collaborate, and alignment around common goals can indicate the strength of team cohesion.

By monitoring team dynamics metrics, managers can identify areas where interventions may be needed to improve communication, collaboration, and overall team effectiveness.

Continuous Improvement Metrics

Continuous improvement metrics focus on tracking progress over time and identifying opportunities for ongoing refinement and enhancement. These metrics are aligned with the principles of continuous improvement and agile methodologies. Examples of continuous improvement metrics include:

- *Cycle Time:* For teams engaged in iterative processes, tracking cycle time (the time taken to complete one iteration or cycle) can help identify opportunities to streamline workflows and increase efficiency.

- *Feedback Loop Closure Time:* Measuring the time it takes for feedback or suggestions to be implemented can highlight the team's responsiveness to input and its ability to adapt quickly.

- *Learning and Development Participation:* Tracking participation in training programs, workshops, or other learning opportunities can indicate the team's commitment to personal and professional growth.

By prioritizing continuous improvement metrics, managers can foster a culture of learning, adaptability, and innovation within the team.

Conclusion

Evaluating team performance metrics is a multifaceted process that requires careful consideration of various factors, including key performance indicators, quality metrics, team dynamics, and continuous improvement initiatives. By leveraging a balanced mix of quantitative and qualitative metrics, managers can gain valuable insights into their team's current state, identify areas for improvement, and ultimately drive higher levels of performance and success.

In the next sections, we will delve deeper into identifying strengths and weaknesses within the team and conducting skills assessments to further enhance team effectiveness and productivity.

2.2 Identifying Strengths and Weaknesses

Identifying the strengths and weaknesses of your team is a critical step in the process of building a high-performance team. Understanding what your team excels at and where they may struggle provides valuable insights that can guide your efforts in maximizing their potential and addressing any areas of improvement. In this section, we will explore various strategies and techniques for effectively identifying the strengths and weaknesses of your team.

1. Conducting Skills Inventories:

One of the most straightforward approaches to identifying strengths and weaknesses is by conducting a comprehensive skills inventory of your team members. A skills inventory involves systematically cataloging the skills, competencies, and capabilities possessed by each team member. This can include technical skills, soft skills, domain expertise, and specialized knowledge relevant to their roles within the team.

To conduct a skills inventory, you can utilize various methods such as self-assessment surveys, one-on-one interviews, or peer evaluations. Encourage team members to reflect on their own strengths and weaknesses honestly and provide specific examples or evidence to support their assessments. Additionally, gathering feedback from colleagues and supervisors can offer valuable perspectives on individual strengths and areas for development.

Once you have compiled the data from the skills inventory, analyze the results to identify common strengths shared by multiple team members as well as any notable gaps or deficiencies. This information serves as a foundation for designing targeted development plans and allocating resources effectively to address skill gaps within the team.

2. Performance Reviews and Feedback:

Performance reviews provide an opportunity to assess the strengths and weaknesses of individual team members in the context of their job responsibilities and performance objectives. Regular feedback sessions, whether formal or informal, allow managers to evaluate performance, provide constructive criticism, and recognize achievements.

During performance reviews, focus on specific performance metrics, goals, and key performance indicators (KPIs) relevant to each team member's role. Evaluate their performance against predefined criteria and benchmarks, highlighting areas of excellence and areas needing improvement. Encourage open dialogue and active listening to ensure that team members feel empowered to share their perspectives and seek clarification or support as needed.

In addition to managerial feedback, peer feedback can offer valuable insights into an individual's strengths and weaknesses from the perspective of their colleagues. Peer reviews or 360-degree feedback surveys allow team members to provide feedback anonymously, promoting honesty and candor in assessing each other's performance. Consider incorporating peer feedback as part of the performance review process to gain a comprehensive understanding of individual contributions within the team.

3. Observational Assessment:

Observational assessment involves closely observing team members in action to evaluate their skills, behaviors, and interactions within the team environment. As a manager, actively engage with your team during meetings, collaborative projects, and day-to-day activities to gain firsthand insights into their strengths and weaknesses.

Pay attention to how team members communicate, collaborate, problem-solve, and handle challenges in real-time situations. Observe their level of engagement, initiative, creativity, and ability to adapt to changing circumstances. Take note of any recurring patterns or trends in behavior and performance that may indicate areas of strength or areas needing improvement.

In addition to direct observation, leverage opportunities for informal conversations and casual interactions with team members to gather qualitative feedback and impressions. Encourage open communication and create a supportive environment where team members feel comfortable sharing their perspectives and concerns openly.

4. Psychometric Assessments:

Psychometric assessments are standardized tools and techniques used to measure individual characteristics, personality traits, cognitive abilities, and behavioral preferences. These assessments provide objective data and insights into the strengths and weaknesses of team members, complementing subjective observations and feedback.

There are various types of psychometric assessments available, including personality assessments, emotional intelligence assessments, cognitive ability tests, and leadership assessments. Administering psychometric assessments can help uncover hidden talents, identify potential areas for development, and facilitate more informed decision-making in team selection, role assignments, and performance management.

When using psychometric assessments, ensure that they are administered ethically and interpreted appropriately by qualified professionals. Provide clear explanations of the purpose and significance of the assessments to team members and assure them that the results will be used constructively to support their growth and development.

5. SWOT Analysis:

A SWOT analysis is a strategic planning tool used to evaluate the strengths, weaknesses, opportunities, and threats facing an organization or team. Conducting a SWOT analysis enables you to systematically assess internal factors (strengths and weaknesses) and external factors (opportunities and threats) that impact team performance and effectiveness.

To conduct a SWOT analysis for your team, gather input from team members through brainstorming sessions or structured discussions. Identify specific strengths that differentiate your team from others, such as specialized skills, diverse expertise, or strong collaboration. Likewise, identify weaknesses or areas where your team may be at a disadvantage, such as skill gaps, communication barriers, or resource constraints.

Next, analyze external factors that present opportunities for your team to excel, such as emerging trends, market demand, or potential partnerships. Similarly, identify potential threats or challenges that may hinder your team's success, such as competition, technological disruptions, or regulatory changes.

Once you have completed the SWOT analysis, use the insights gained to develop strategies for leveraging strengths, addressing weaknesses, capitalizing on opportunities, and mitigating threats. Incorporate these strategies into your team's action plans and initiatives to enhance performance and achieve strategic objectives.

Conclusion:

Identifying the strengths and weaknesses of your team is a dynamic and ongoing process that requires a combination of objective assessment methods, qualitative feedback, and strategic analysis. By taking a comprehensive approach to assessment, you can gain deeper insights into your team's capabilities, foster a culture of continuous improvement, and position your team for success in achieving its goals. Remember to communicate findings transparently, involve team members in the assessment process, and prioritize actions that maximize strengths and address weaknesses effectively. With a clear understanding of your team's current state, you can guide them towards higher levels of performance and collaboration, driving sustained success in the long term.

2.3 Conducting Team Member Skills Assessment

Conducting a comprehensive skills assessment of your team members is a crucial step in understanding the capabilities and potential areas for improvement within your team. Skill assessments provide valuable insights into individual strengths, weaknesses, and development opportunities, enabling you to tailor strategies for maximizing team performance. In this section, we will explore the process of conducting a thorough team member skills assessment, including methodologies, tools, and best practices.

Understanding the Importance of Skills Assessment

Before delving into the practical aspects of conducting a skills assessment, it's essential to grasp why this process holds significance for team performance and organizational success. A skill assessment serves multiple purposes:

1. Identifying Strengths: By assessing the skills possessed by each team member, you can identify areas of expertise and proficiency. Recognizing individual strengths enables you to leverage them effectively within the team.

2. Highlighting Weaknesses: Pinpointing areas where team members may lack necessary skills or competencies allows you to address these deficiencies through targeted training and development initiatives.

3. Promoting Collaboration: Understanding the skills distribution within the team facilitates better collaboration and task allocation. Matching tasks with individuals possessing the relevant skills enhances efficiency and productivity.

4. Informing Recruitment and Succession Planning: Skill assessments provide valuable data for recruitment decisions and succession planning. Knowing the skills gap within the team helps in identifying the type of talent required to fill those gaps and groom future leaders.

Methods of Skills Assessment

Several methods can be employed to assess the skills of team members, each with its advantages and limitations. The choice of method depends on factors such as team size, available resources, and organizational culture. Here are some common methods:

1. Self-Assessment: In this method, team members evaluate their own skills and competencies based on predefined criteria. Self-assessment can provide valuable insights into how individuals perceive their abilities, although it may be subjective and influenced by personal biases.

2. Peer Assessment: Peer assessment involves team members evaluating each other's skills and providing feedback. This method promotes peer learning and collaboration, but it may also be prone to biases and conflicts of interest.

3. Manager Assessment: Managers assess the skills of their team members based on their observations, interactions, and performance evaluations. Manager assessment offers an objective perspective and aligns with organizational goals but may lack insights into individual nuances.

4. Skills Testing: Skills testing involves administering tests, quizzes, or simulations to assess specific technical or functional skills. This method provides objective data on individual capabilities but may not capture soft skills or behavioral competencies effectively.

5. 360-Degree Feedback: 360-degree feedback solicits input from multiple sources, including peers, subordinates, supervisors, and self-assessment. This comprehensive approach offers a well-rounded view of an individual's skills and behavior, fostering holistic development.

Best Practices for Conducting Skills Assessment

To ensure the effectiveness and fairness of the skills assessment process, it's essential to adhere to best practices:

1. Establish Clear Criteria: Define the skills and competencies relevant to the team's objectives and roles. Clear criteria provide a framework for assessment and ensure consistency across evaluations.

2. Use Multiple Methods: Combine different assessment methods to gain a comprehensive understanding of team members' skills. Incorporating self-assessment, peer feedback, and manager assessment provides a balanced perspective.

3. Ensure Confidentiality and Anonymity: Encourage honesty and transparency by guaranteeing confidentiality and anonymity in feedback processes. This enables team members to provide candid assessments without fear of reprisal.

4. Provide Feedback and Development Opportunities: Share assessment results with team members and offer constructive feedback. Identify areas for improvement and collaborate on creating development plans to enhance skills and competencies.

5. Regular Review and Update: Skills assessment is not a one-time activity but an ongoing process. Review and update assessments periodically to reflect changes in team dynamics, roles, and organizational priorities.

Conclusion

Conducting a team member skills assessment is a fundamental aspect of building high-performance teams. By systematically evaluating individual skills and competencies, managers can identify strengths, address weaknesses, and optimize team dynamics. Leveraging a variety of assessment methods and adhering to best practices ensures fairness, accuracy, and alignment with organizational objectives. Ultimately, investing in skills assessment contributes to the development of a skilled and cohesive team capable of achieving collective success.

3. Setting Clear Team Goals and Objectives

3.1 Defining SMART Goals for Your Team

In the pursuit of organizational excellence, setting clear and achievable goals is paramount. These goals serve as guiding lights, directing the efforts of individual team members towards a unified purpose. However, the mere act of setting goals is not enough; they must be SMART—Specific, Measurable, Achievable, Relevant, and Time-bound. This section delves into the intricacies of crafting SMART goals for your team, ensuring alignment with broader organizational objectives and maximizing the potential for success.

The Essence of SMART Goals

SMART is not just an acronym; it encapsulates the fundamental characteristics that distinguish effective goals from vague aspirations. Let's dissect each element to understand its significance:

Specific

Specificity injects clarity into goals, leaving no room for ambiguity. Instead of a broad objective like "increase sales," a specific goal could be "increase sales revenue by 15% in the next quarter." This precision provides a clear target for team members to work towards, enhancing focus and accountability.

Measurable

Measurability enables teams to gauge progress objectively. Without measurable metrics, it's challenging to determine whether goals have been achieved or if adjustments are necessary. Utilizing quantifiable indicators such as revenue figures, customer satisfaction scores, or project completion rates facilitates accurate assessment and informed decision-making.

Achievable

While ambition is commendable, setting unattainable goals can demoralize teams and undermine motivation. Achievability necessitates a balance between ambition and realism. Goals should stretch team members to reach their full potential without veering into the realm of impossibility. Conducting a thorough assessment of resources, capabilities, and external factors is essential in determining feasibility.

Relevant

Relevance ensures that goals are aligned with organizational priorities and contribute meaningfully to the overarching mission. Each goal should serve a purpose, advancing the organization towards its desired outcomes. Contextual relevance fosters a sense of purpose among team members, fostering intrinsic motivation and commitment to goal attainment.

Time-bound

Setting a deadline instills a sense of urgency and imparts a tangible sense of direction. Without temporal constraints, goals risk languishing indefinitely, overshadowed by more immediate concerns. Establishing clear timelines cultivates a sense of accountability and enables teams to prioritize tasks effectively. However, deadlines should be realistic, allowing sufficient time for thorough planning and execution.

Implementing SMART Goals

Crafting SMART goals requires a systematic approach, encompassing collaborative brainstorming, strategic alignment, and meticulous planning. The following steps outline a comprehensive framework for implementing SMART goals within your team:

Step 1: Collaborative Goal Setting

Effective goal setting is a collaborative endeavor that leverages the collective wisdom and expertise of team members. Encourage open dialogue and brainstorming sessions to generate ideas and insights. Solicit input from diverse perspectives to ensure comprehensive goal coverage and foster a sense of ownership among team members.

Step 2: Strategic Alignment

Alignment with organizational objectives is paramount to ensure coherence and synergy across departments and teams. Regularly review organizational priorities and strategic initiatives to identify areas where team goals can contribute most effectively. Aligning team goals with broader strategic imperatives enhances organizational agility and facilitates seamless integration into overarching plans.

Step 3: Defining Metrics and Benchmarks

Translate overarching goals into actionable metrics and benchmarks that facilitate monitoring and evaluation. Select metrics that are relevant, reliable, and reflective of progress towards goal attainment. Establish baseline measurements to provide context and set realistic targets that challenge but do not overwhelm team members.

Step 4: Assigning Responsibilities

Clarify roles and responsibilities to ensure accountability and foster a sense of ownership among team members. Clearly delineate who is responsible for each aspect of goal implementation, including task execution, progress monitoring, and performance evaluation. Encourage autonomy and initiative while providing necessary support and resources to facilitate success.

Step 5: Monitoring and Adjusting

Regular monitoring is essential to track progress, identify obstacles, and make timely adjustments as needed. Establish checkpoints and review mechanisms to assess progress against predetermined milestones. Encourage proactive communication and transparency to facilitate early detection of issues and prompt resolution. Be prepared to adapt goals and strategies in response to changing circumstances or emerging opportunities.

Conclusion

In summary, setting SMART goals is a cornerstone of effective team management, providing a roadmap for success and fostering alignment with organizational objectives. By adhering to the principles of specificity, measurability, achievability, relevance, and time-bound nature, teams can optimize their performance and achieve tangible results. Through collaborative goal setting, strategic alignment, and proactive monitoring, managers can empower their teams to excel and contribute meaningfully to the organization's success.

3.2 Aligning Team Goals with Organizational Objectives

Aligning team goals with organizational objectives is a critical aspect of building high-performance teams. When team goals are closely aligned with the broader mission and vision of the organization, it fosters cohesion, enhances productivity, and drives overall success. In this section, we will delve deeper into the strategies and best practices for effectively aligning team goals with organizational objectives.

Understanding Organizational Objectives

Before delving into aligning team goals, it's imperative to have a clear understanding of the organizational objectives. These objectives typically stem from the organization's mission statement, strategic plans, and key performance indicators (KPIs). Organizational objectives can encompass various aspects, including financial targets, market expansion goals, customer satisfaction metrics, innovation initiatives, and more.

Importance of Alignment

Alignment between team goals and organizational objectives is vital for several reasons:

1. Strategic Focus: When team goals are aligned with organizational objectives, it ensures that every effort contributes directly to the overarching strategic priorities of the organization.

2. Motivation and Engagement: Employees are more motivated and engaged when they understand how their work aligns with the broader organizational goals. It provides them with a sense of purpose and direction.

3. Resource Allocation: Aligning goals helps in optimizing resource allocation by directing time, budget, and manpower towards initiatives that drive the most significant impact on organizational success.

4. Clarity and Transparency: Clear alignment fosters transparency and clarity within the organization, minimizing confusion and promoting a unified approach towards achieving common objectives.

Strategies for Alignment

Achieving alignment between team goals and organizational objectives requires a systematic approach and effective communication. Here are some strategies to facilitate this alignment:

1. Cascade Objectives Downward: Start by cascading organizational objectives downward to teams and individual employees. Break down overarching goals into smaller, actionable targets that each team can contribute to.

2. Collaborative Goal Setting: Involve team members in the goal-setting process to ensure buy-in and commitment. Encourage teams to propose goals that align with organizational objectives while leveraging their expertise and insights.

3. Regular Alignment Meetings: Schedule regular alignment meetings where teams can review progress, discuss challenges, and realign goals if necessary. These meetings serve as checkpoints to ensure that team objectives remain aligned with evolving organizational priorities.

4. Performance Metrics Alignment: Align performance metrics and KPIs at the team level with those of the broader organization. Ensure that teams understand how their performance will be measured and evaluated in relation to organizational objectives.

5. Cross-Functional Collaboration: Foster collaboration and communication between different teams and departments to ensure alignment across the organization. Encourage cross-functional projects and initiatives that support shared objectives.

6. Continuous Communication: Maintain open and transparent communication channels to keep teams informed about organizational goals, changes in priorities, and strategic shifts. Provide regular updates and feedback to reinforce alignment.

Overcoming Challenges

Despite the importance of alignment, several challenges may hinder the process. These challenges include:

1. Lack of Clarity: Unclear organizational objectives or miscommunication can lead to confusion and ambiguity at the team level.

2. Conflicting Priorities: Teams may face conflicting priorities, especially in matrix organizations or during periods of change.

3. Resistance to Change: Some team members may resist aligning their goals with organizational objectives due to fear of change or uncertainty about the implications.

4. Silos and Communication Barriers: Siloed organizational structures and communication barriers can hinder collaboration and alignment across teams and departments.

To overcome these challenges, it's essential to emphasize the importance of alignment, provide clarity and guidance, address concerns proactively, and foster a culture of collaboration and adaptability.

Case Study: Successful Alignment in Action

To illustrate the benefits of alignment, let's examine a case study of a company that successfully aligned its team goals with organizational objectives:

Company XYZ: Company XYZ, a leading technology firm, aimed to expand its market presence globally while maintaining a focus on innovation and customer satisfaction. To achieve this, the company's leadership emphasized the importance of alignment at all levels of the organization.

- *Cascade of Objectives:* The executive team cascaded strategic objectives, such as market expansion targets and innovation initiatives, to each department and team within the organization.

- *Collaborative Goal Setting:* Teams were encouraged to participate in the goal-setting process, leveraging their domain expertise to propose objectives that aligned with the company's strategic priorities.

- *Regular Alignment Meetings:* Quarterly alignment meetings were scheduled, where teams reviewed progress, identified challenges, and adjusted goals as needed to stay aligned with evolving market dynamics.

- *Performance Metrics Alignment:* Key performance indicators, such as revenue growth, customer satisfaction scores, and product innovation metrics, were aligned across all levels of the organization to ensure consistency and accountability.

As a result of these efforts, Company XYZ experienced significant growth in both revenue and market share, while maintaining high levels of employee engagement and customer satisfaction. The clear alignment of team goals with organizational objectives played a pivotal role in driving this success.

Conclusion

Aligning team goals with organizational objectives is not just a managerial task; it's a strategic imperative for organizational success. By ensuring that every team's efforts are directed towards common objectives, organizations can maximize productivity, enhance employee engagement, and achieve sustainable growth. Through collaborative goal setting, regular communication, and a focus on shared metrics, organizations can overcome challenges and foster a culture of alignment and accountability. Remember, alignment is not a one-time exercise but an ongoing process that requires continuous effort and commitment from all stakeholders.

3.3 Communicating Goals Effectively to Team Members

Effective communication of team goals is paramount to the success of any endeavor. Without clear and consistent communication, team members may misunderstand their objectives, leading to inefficiencies, missed deadlines, and ultimately, project failure. In this section, we will explore various strategies and best practices for communicating goals effectively to team members.

1. Establishing a Communication Plan

A communication plan is essential for ensuring that team goals are effectively communicated to all members. This plan should outline who will communicate the goals, how often communication will occur, and through which channels. By establishing a clear communication plan upfront, managers can avoid confusion and ensure that every team member receives the necessary information.

2. Utilizing Multiple Channels

Different team members may prefer different communication channels, so it's essential to utilize a variety of methods to ensure everyone receives the message. This could include in-person meetings, emails, instant messaging platforms, project management software, or even visual aids such as charts or graphs. By using multiple channels, managers can reach a broader audience and increase the likelihood that team members will understand the goals.

3. Tailoring Communication to the Audience

Not all team members will have the same level of understanding or interest in the project goals. Therefore, it's essential to tailor communication to the specific audience. For example, while some team members may appreciate detailed explanations and data-driven presentations, others may prefer concise summaries or visual representations. By understanding the preferences and needs of each team member, managers can ensure that communication is both effective and engaging.

4. Providing Context

Simply stating the goals without providing context can lead to confusion or resistance from team members. It's crucial to explain why these goals are important, how they align with the organization's objectives, and what impact they will have on the team and its stakeholders. Providing context helps team members understand the bigger picture and fosters a sense of purpose and motivation.

5. Encouraging Feedback and Questions

Communication should be a two-way street, with opportunities for team members to ask questions, seek clarification, and provide feedback. Managers should create an environment where team members feel comfortable expressing their thoughts and concerns openly. By encouraging feedback and questions, managers can identify any misunderstandings early on and address them proactively.

6. Setting Milestones and Checkpoints

Breaking down larger goals into smaller milestones and checkpoints can help keep team members focused and motivated. Communicating these milestones clearly and regularly reinforces the progress being made and allows for adjustments if necessary. Additionally, setting deadlines for each milestone helps create a sense of urgency and accountability among team members.

7. Celebrating Successes

Recognition and celebration are powerful motivators for teams. When goals are achieved, it's essential to acknowledge the hard work and dedication of team members. This could involve a simple thank-you message, a team outing, or even rewards or incentives for exceptional performance. Celebrating successes not only boosts morale but also reinforces the importance of working towards common goals.

8. Being Transparent

Transparency is key to building trust within a team. Managers should be transparent about the goals, progress, challenges, and decision-making processes. When team members feel that they are kept in the loop and their input is valued, they are more likely to be engaged and committed to achieving the goals.

9. Monitoring and Adjusting Communication

Effective communication is an ongoing process that requires monitoring and adjustment. Managers should regularly assess the effectiveness of their communication strategies and be willing to adapt them as needed. This could involve soliciting feedback from team members, conducting communication audits, or seeking input from other stakeholders. By continuously improving communication practices, managers can ensure that team goals are understood and pursued effectively.

Example: Setting Clear Team Goals and Objectives

Let's consider a software development company, "TechSprint," that is embarking on a new project to develop a mobile application for tracking personal finances. The project team consists of developers, designers, quality assurance testers, and a project manager. The goal is to create a user-friendly app that allows individuals to easily track their expenses, set budgets, and receive financial insights.

Step 1: Defining the Goal

The project manager initiates the goal-setting process by convening a team meeting. During this meeting, the team collectively defines the overarching goal: to develop a feature-rich mobile application for personal finance management that meets the needs of modern users.

Step 2: Breaking Down the Goal

Next, the team breaks down the overarching goal into specific objectives:

- Objective 1: Develop a user-friendly interface for easy navigation and intuitive use.

- Objective 2: Implement secure authentication and data encryption to protect users' financial information.

- Objective 3: Integrate features for expense tracking, budget setting, and financial reporting.

- Objective 4: Conduct rigorous testing to ensure the app's functionality, reliability, and security.

- Objective 5: Launch the app on major app stores and achieve a high user adoption rate within the first three months.

Step 3: Making Goals SMART

To ensure that the objectives are SMART (Specific, Measurable, Achievable, Relevant, Time-bound), the project manager works with the team to refine them further:

- Specific: Each objective clearly outlines what needs to be achieved.

- Measurable: Success criteria are defined for each objective, allowing progress to be tracked.

- Achievable: Objectives are realistic and within the team's capabilities.

- Relevant: Objectives align with the overall goal of developing a personal finance management app.

- Time-bound: Deadlines are set for each objective to ensure timely completion.

Step 4: Aligning Goals with Organizational Objectives

The project manager communicates the team's goals to upper management to ensure alignment with the company's broader objectives. This ensures that the project contributes to the company's strategic vision and mission.

Step 5: Communicating Goals to Team Members

The project manager utilizes various communication channels to ensure that all team members understand the goals and objectives:

- In-person kick-off meeting: The project manager hosts a kick-off meeting to present the goals and objectives to the entire team. This allows for interactive discussions and clarifications.
- Email follow-up: The project manager sends a detailed email summarizing the goals and objectives discussed during the meeting. This serves as a reference for team members to revisit when needed.
- Project management software: The goals and objectives are documented in the project management software used by the team. This ensures that they are easily accessible and visible to everyone involved in the project.

Step 6: Monitoring Progress and Adjusting Goals

Throughout the project, the project manager monitors progress towards each objective and adjusts goals as necessary. Regular team meetings are held to review progress, address challenges, and make any necessary course corrections to keep the project on track.

Example: Setting Clear Team Goals and Objectives

Let's take the example of a marketing agency, "MarketMinds," tasked with launching a new advertising campaign for a client in the fitness industry. The project team comprises marketing strategists, creative designers, copywriters, social media managers, and account managers. The goal is to create a compelling and engaging advertising campaign that drives brand awareness and increases customer engagement for the client's new line of fitness products.

Step 1: Defining the Goal

The project manager initiates a brainstorming session with the team to define the overarching goal: to launch a successful advertising campaign that effectively promotes the client's fitness products and resonates with the target audience.

Step 2: Breaking Down the Goal

The team collaboratively breaks down the overarching goal into specific objectives:

- Objective 1: Conduct market research to understand the target audience's demographics, preferences, and behaviors.

- Objective 2: Develop creative concepts and visual assets that communicate the brand message and product benefits effectively.

- Objective 3: Create engaging copy and messaging for various advertising channels, including social media, print, and digital platforms.

- Objective 4: Implement a comprehensive advertising strategy that utilizes a mix of channels, including social media ads, influencer partnerships, and email marketing campaigns.

- Objective 5: Monitor campaign performance and analyze key metrics to measure success, such as reach, engagement, and conversion rates.

Step 3: Making Goals SMART

The project manager ensures that each objective is SMART:

- Specific: Objectives clearly outline what needs to be accomplished.

- Measurable: Success criteria are defined for each objective, allowing progress to be quantified and evaluated.

- Achievable: Objectives are realistic and attainable within the project's constraints and resources.

- Relevant: Objectives align with the overall goal of launching a successful advertising campaign for the client's fitness products.

- Time-bound: Deadlines are set for each objective to ensure timely execution and completion.

Step 4: Aligning Goals with Organizational Objectives

The project manager communicates the team's goals to senior management and the client to ensure alignment with the company's objectives and the client's expectations. This ensures that the campaign contributes to the client's marketing objectives and business goals.

Step 5: Communicating Goals to Team Members

The project manager employs various communication methods to ensure that all team members understand the goals and objectives:

- Team meeting: The project manager hosts a team meeting to present the goals and objectives, encourage collaboration, and address any questions or concerns.

- Project management software: The goals and objectives are documented in the project management software used by the team, providing a centralized source of information and accountability.

- Weekly progress updates: The project manager sends out weekly progress updates via email or team collaboration platforms, highlighting achievements, upcoming milestones, and any adjustments to the plan.

Step 6: Monitoring Progress and Adjusting Goals

Throughout the campaign, the project manager monitors progress towards each objective and makes adjustments as needed based on feedback, performance data, and changing circumstances. Regular team meetings and performance reviews are conducted to assess progress, address challenges, and make strategic decisions to optimize campaign performance.

Conclusion

Effective communication of team goals is essential for driving success and achieving desired outcomes. By establishing clear communication plans, utilizing multiple channels, tailoring communication to the audience, providing context, encouraging feedback, setting milestones, celebrating successes, being transparent, and monitoring and adjusting communication, managers can ensure that team members are aligned, engaged, and motivated to work towards common objectives. Ultimately, effective communication fosters collaboration, trust, and high-performance within teams.

4. Establishing Team Norms and Expectations

4.1 Defining Team Norms and Core Values

Establishing clear norms and core values is foundational to the success of any team. Norms are the agreed-upon behaviors, attitudes, and expectations that guide team members' interactions and performance. Core values, on the other hand, are the fundamental beliefs and principles that define the team's identity and guide its decision-making processes. In this section, we will delve into the importance of defining team norms and core values and explore effective strategies for doing so.

Importance of Team Norms and Core Values

Clear team norms and core values serve as the bedrock upon which a high-performing team is built. They provide a framework for behavior and decision-making, fostering cohesion, trust, and accountability among team members. Here are several reasons why defining team norms and core values is crucial:

1. Alignment: Norms and core values ensure that team members are aligned with the overarching goals and objectives of the team and the organization. When everyone is working towards a common set of principles, collaboration becomes more effective, and conflicts are minimized.

2. Behavioral Expectations: Norms outline the expected behaviors and interactions within the team. By establishing guidelines for communication, collaboration, and conflict resolution, team norms promote a positive and productive work environment.

3. Accountability: Clear norms and core values create a culture of accountability where team members hold themselves and each other responsible for their actions and contributions. This accountability fosters a sense of ownership and commitment to the team's success.

4. Decision-Making: Core values serve as a guidepost for decision-making, helping team members make choices that are in alignment with the team's principles and objectives. When faced with tough decisions, referring back to core values can provide clarity and direction.

5. Cohesion and Trust: Norms and core values strengthen team cohesion and trust by fostering a sense of belonging and shared purpose. When individuals feel valued and respected within the team, they are more likely to collaborate effectively and support one another.

Strategies for Defining Team Norms and Core Values

Defining team norms and core values is a collaborative process that involves active participation from all team members. Here are some strategies for effectively establishing norms and core values within your team:

1. Facilitated Discussions: Schedule team meetings or workshops dedicated to discussing and defining team norms and core values. Encourage open and honest dialogue where team members can express their thoughts, concerns, and aspirations freely.

2. Brainstorming Sessions: Conduct brainstorming sessions where team members generate ideas for potential norms and core values based on the team's goals, objectives, and culture. Encourage creativity and exploration during these sessions.

3. Consensus Building: Work towards consensus when identifying and finalizing team norms and core values. Seek input from all team members and strive to reach agreements that reflect the collective values and priorities of the team.

4. Documentation: Once team norms and core values have been established, document them in a clear and accessible format. This could be in the form of a team charter, mission statement, or code of conduct that outlines the agreed-upon norms and values.

5. Reinforcement: Continuously reinforce and uphold team norms and core values through regular communication, feedback, and recognition. Celebrate instances where team members exemplify these principles and address any deviations promptly and constructively.

6. Evaluation and Adjustment: Periodically evaluate the effectiveness of team norms and core values and be open to making adjustments as needed. As the team evolves and faces new challenges, revisiting and refining norms and values ensures their continued relevance and impact.

Case Study: Defining Team Norms and Core Values at Company XYZ

To illustrate the importance of defining team norms and core values, let's examine a case study involving Company XYZ, a fast-growing tech startup.

Background: Company XYZ recently formed a new cross-functional team tasked with developing a groundbreaking product within a tight timeline. Recognizing the importance of establishing clear norms and core values from the outset, the team embarked on a collaborative process to define these guiding principles.

Process: The team began by holding a series of facilitated discussions and brainstorming sessions where team members shared their perspectives on what values were most important to them and how they wanted to work together. Through open dialogue and consensus building, the team identified the following core values:

1. Innovation: We embrace creativity and strive to push the boundaries of what's possible.

2. Collaboration: We believe in the power of teamwork and actively seek opportunities to support and learn from one another.

3. Integrity: We uphold honesty, transparency, and ethical behavior in all of our interactions.

4. Accountability: We take ownership of our work and hold ourselves and each other accountable for delivering results.

5. Customer-Centricity: We prioritize the needs and experiences of our customers in everything we do.

Outcome: By defining these core values, the team created a shared understanding of the behaviors and attitudes expected of all members. These values served as a guiding compass, steering the team through challenges and decisions with confidence and cohesion. As a result, the team successfully launched the product ahead of schedule and received positive feedback from both internal stakeholders and external customers.

Conclusion

In conclusion, defining team norms and core values is a critical step towards building a high-performance team. By establishing clear expectations and guiding principles, teams can foster a culture of collaboration, accountability, and innovation that drives success. Through collaborative discussions, consensus building, and ongoing reinforcement, teams can ensure that their norms and core values remain relevant and impactful in the face of evolving challenges and opportunities.

4.2 Establishing Clear Expectations for Team Members

Setting clear expectations is a cornerstone of effective team management. When team members know exactly what is expected of them, they are better equipped to perform their roles effectively and contribute to the team's overall success. However, establishing clear expectations involves more than just outlining tasks and responsibilities; it requires thoughtful communication, alignment with organizational goals, and ongoing feedback. In this section, we will explore strategies for defining and communicating expectations to ensure clarity and alignment within the team.

1. Defining Roles and Responsibilities

The first step in establishing clear expectations is defining each team member's roles and responsibilities. This involves identifying the specific tasks, projects, and objectives that each team member is accountable for. By clearly outlining these expectations, team members can understand their individual contributions to the team's goals and how their work aligns with the broader objectives of the organization.

To define roles and responsibilities effectively, managers should:

- Conduct a thorough assessment of the team's needs and objectives.

- Identify each team member's strengths, skills, and areas for growth.

- Delegate tasks based on individual capabilities and interests.

- Clearly communicate expectations regarding deadlines, quality standards, and deliverables.

By providing clarity around roles and responsibilities, managers empower team members to take ownership of their work and collaborate more effectively with their peers.

2. Aligning Expectations with Organizational Goals

In addition to defining individual roles and responsibilities, it is essential to align team expectations with the broader goals and objectives of the organization. When team members understand how their work contributes to the achievement of organizational targets, they are more motivated and engaged in their roles.

To align expectations with organizational goals, managers should:

- Clearly communicate the organization's mission, vision, and strategic priorities.
- Help team members understand how their work directly supports these objectives.
- Encourage collaboration and cross-functional communication to ensure alignment across teams.
- Provide regular updates and feedback on the organization's progress towards its goals.

By aligning team expectations with organizational goals, managers create a sense of purpose and direction that inspires team members to perform at their best.

3. Establishing Performance Metrics and Standards

Clear expectations should be accompanied by measurable performance metrics and standards to assess progress and provide feedback. Performance metrics help quantify individual and team contributions, identify areas for improvement, and track progress towards goals. Additionally, establishing clear standards for quality and performance ensures consistency and accountability across the team.

When establishing performance metrics and standards, managers should:

- Define key performance indicators (KPIs) that align with team objectives and organizational goals.
- Set realistic targets and benchmarks for performance improvement.

- Provide regular feedback and coaching to help team members meet or exceed performance expectations.

- Recognize and celebrate achievements to reinforce positive behaviors and outcomes.

By establishing performance metrics and standards, managers create a culture of accountability and continuous improvement within the team.

4. Communicating Expectations Effectively

Effective communication is essential for ensuring that team members understand and internalize expectations. Managers should utilize various communication channels and techniques to convey information clearly and consistently. This includes one-on-one meetings, team meetings, email updates, and project management tools.

When communicating expectations, managers should:

- Be transparent and honest about goals, priorities, and challenges.

- Encourage open dialogue and feedback to address any concerns or misunderstandings.

- Adapt communication styles to meet the needs of different team members.

- Provide regular updates and reminders to reinforce expectations and priorities.

By fostering a culture of open communication, managers can ensure that team members feel informed, supported, and empowered to meet expectations.

5. Monitoring and Adjusting Expectations as Needed

Finally, establishing clear expectations is an ongoing process that requires regular monitoring and adjustment. As team dynamics, priorities, and objectives evolve, managers must be flexible and responsive to change. This may involve revisiting and updating expectations, reallocating resources, or providing additional support and guidance as needed.

To monitor and adjust expectations effectively, managers should:

- Solicit feedback from team members on their experiences and challenges.
- Assess progress towards goals and objectives on a regular basis.
- Identify any discrepancies or gaps between expectations and reality.
- Collaborate with team members to address issues and make necessary adjustments.

By staying proactive and adaptable, managers can ensure that expectations remain relevant and achievable in the face of changing circumstances.

Conclusion

Establishing clear expectations is fundamental to building high-performance teams. By defining roles and responsibilities, aligning expectations with organizational goals, establishing performance metrics and standards, communicating effectively, and monitoring progress, managers can create a culture of clarity, accountability, and excellence within their teams. By empowering team members to understand their roles, responsibilities, and contributions, managers lay the foundation for success and foster a sense of ownership and commitment that drives performance and results.

4.3 Encouraging Accountability and Responsibility

Encouraging accountability and responsibility within a team is essential for its success. When team members feel a sense of ownership over their tasks and outcomes, they are more likely to be motivated, engaged, and committed to achieving collective goals. However, fostering accountability and responsibility is not always straightforward and requires a combination of leadership strategies, effective communication, and creating a supportive team culture. In this section, we will explore various approaches managers can take to promote accountability and responsibility within their teams.

Setting Clear Expectations

Clear expectations are the foundation of accountability. Team members need to understand what is expected of them in terms of goals, deadlines, quality standards, and roles within the team. Managers should communicate these expectations explicitly and ensure that they are understood by everyone. This can be achieved through individual meetings, team meetings, written documents, or performance reviews. When expectations are clear, team members know what they are accountable for, which reduces ambiguity and confusion.

Empowering Team Members

Empowering team members involves giving them the autonomy and authority to make decisions and take ownership of their work. When individuals feel empowered, they are more likely to demonstrate initiative, creativity, and a sense of responsibility. Managers can empower their team members by delegating tasks, providing resources and support, and trusting them to make the right decisions. Empowerment fosters a culture of accountability where individuals take pride in their work and are motivated to deliver results.

Providing Regular Feedback

Feedback is a powerful tool for promoting accountability and responsibility. It allows managers to recognize and reinforce positive behaviors, address issues promptly, and guide team members towards improvement. Feedback should be specific, timely, and constructive, focusing on both achievements and areas for development. Regular feedback sessions, one-on-one meetings, and performance evaluations provide opportunities for managers to communicate expectations, clarify goals, and support individual growth. By giving and receiving feedback openly, team members become more accountable for their actions and outcomes.

Cultivating a Culture of Ownership

A culture of ownership is one where every team member feels personally invested in the success of the team. Managers play a crucial role in cultivating this culture by fostering a sense of belonging, pride, and shared purpose. This can be achieved through team-building activities, recognition programs, and celebrating achievements collectively. Managers should also encourage open communication, collaboration, and problem-solving, empowering team members to take ownership of both their individual contributions and the overall team's performance. When individuals feel a sense of ownership, they are more likely to hold themselves and their peers accountable for delivering results.

Leading by Example

Leadership by example is perhaps the most powerful way to promote accountability and responsibility within a team. Managers need to demonstrate the behaviors and values they expect from their team members, serving as role models for accountability, integrity, and professionalism. This means taking ownership of mistakes, honoring commitments, and holding oneself accountable to the same standards as others. By leading by example, managers inspire trust, confidence, and respect, creating a positive environment where accountability becomes a natural part of the team culture.

Addressing Accountability Issues

Despite efforts to promote accountability, challenges may arise within teams, such as missed deadlines, low performance, or lack of follow-through. In such cases, it is essential for managers to address accountability issues promptly and constructively. This may involve having candid conversations with individuals to understand the root causes of the problem, providing additional support or resources if needed, and establishing clear consequences for repeated failures to meet expectations. Managers should approach accountability issues with empathy, fairness, and a focus on finding solutions rather than assigning blame. By addressing accountability issues effectively, managers can reinforce expectations, restore trust, and help individuals realign their behavior with team goals.

Conclusion

Encouraging accountability and responsibility is a continuous process that requires commitment, consistency, and adaptability. By setting clear expectations, empowering team members, providing regular feedback, cultivating a culture of ownership, leading by example, and addressing accountability issues proactively, managers can create high-performing teams capable of achieving their full potential. Ultimately, fostering accountability and responsibility not only drives individual and team success but also strengthens trust, collaboration, and morale within the organization.

Example: Creating a Collaborative Environment

Imagine a marketing team tasked with launching a new product campaign. To ensure effective collaboration and communication, the team decides on the following norms and core values:

1. Open Communication: Team members agree to share ideas, feedback, and concerns openly and respectfully during meetings and through digital communication channels.

2. Transparency: All project updates, decisions, and changes are communicated promptly to ensure everyone is informed and aligned with the campaign objectives.

3. Accountability: Each team member takes ownership of their tasks and deadlines, holding themselves and others accountable for meeting project milestones.

4. Innovation: The team encourages creative thinking and problem-solving, embracing new ideas and approaches to optimize the campaign's effectiveness.

By defining these norms and core values together, the marketing team creates a supportive environment where trust, collaboration, and innovation thrive, ultimately leading to the successful execution of the campaign.

Establishing Clear Expectations for Team Members

Example: Clarifying Roles and Responsibilities

In a software development team, clarity around roles and responsibilities is crucial to prevent confusion and ensure efficient project delivery. The team establishes clear expectations by:

1. Role Definition: Each team member understands their specific role within the development process, whether it's frontend coding, backend development, quality assurance, or project management.

2. Task Allocation: Tasks are assigned based on individual strengths and expertise, with clear deadlines and priorities communicated to all team members.

3. Communication Channels: Team members know where to seek help or clarification if they encounter challenges, whether through direct communication with colleagues or utilizing project management tools.

By establishing these clear expectations, the software development team minimizes redundancy, maximizes productivity, and fosters a culture of accountability and collaboration.

Encouraging Accountability and Responsibility

Example: Performance Reviews and Recognition

In a sales team, accountability and responsibility are reinforced through regular performance reviews and recognition programs. The team manager conducts quarterly reviews to:

1. Assess Individual Performance: Each salesperson's performance is evaluated based on key metrics such as sales targets, client satisfaction, and contribution to team goals.

2. Provide Constructive Feedback: Feedback sessions focus on strengths, areas for improvement, and actionable steps for personal and professional growth.

3. Recognize Achievements: Outstanding performance is acknowledged publicly, whether through team meetings, newsletters, or company-wide announcements, to reinforce positive behaviors and motivate others.

By incorporating performance reviews and recognition programs into their team culture, the sales team fosters a sense of accountability, drives continuous improvement, and celebrates individual and collective success.

In conclusion, establishing team norms and expectations is essential for creating a cohesive and high-performing team. By defining clear norms and core values, establishing expectations for team members, and encouraging accountability and responsibility, teams can cultivate a positive work environment where trust, collaboration, and success thrive. These principles apply across various industries and team structures, serving as the foundation for effective teamwork and achievement of shared goals.

PART II
Building and Developing Your Team

5. Selecting the Right Team Members

5.1 Identifying Key Competencies and Skills

Identifying the key competencies and skills required for building a high-performance team is an essential step in the process of selecting the right team members. These competencies and skills serve as the foundation upon which the team's success is built. In this section, we will delve into the various aspects of identifying and defining these essential attributes.

Understanding the Role Requirements

Before identifying specific competencies and skills, it's crucial to have a clear understanding of the role's requirements within the team. This involves analyzing the job description, understanding the team's objectives, and determining how the role contributes to achieving those objectives. By gaining clarity on these aspects, managers can pinpoint the competencies and skills necessary for success in the role.

Core Competencies

Core competencies are fundamental skills and characteristics that are essential for success in any role within the team. These competencies typically include:

1. *Communication:* Effective communication is paramount for seamless collaboration within the team. Team members should be able to express their ideas clearly, actively listen to others, and adapt their communication style to different audiences.

2. *Collaboration:* The ability to work collaboratively with others is vital for achieving team goals. This involves being able to share responsibilities, leverage each other's strengths, and resolve conflicts constructively.

3. *Problem-Solving:* High-performance teams are adept at identifying and solving problems efficiently. Team members should possess strong analytical skills, creativity, and the ability to think critically under pressure.

4. *Adaptability:* In today's dynamic work environment, adaptability is crucial. Team members should be able to quickly adjust to changing circumstances, embrace new technologies, and navigate uncertainty with resilience.

5. *Leadership:* Leadership is not limited to individuals in formal leadership positions; it's about taking initiative, inspiring others, and driving positive change. Every team member should demonstrate leadership qualities to some extent.

Role-Specific Skills

In addition to core competencies, role-specific skills are necessary to fulfill the responsibilities of a particular position within the team. These skills may vary depending on the nature of the role, but some common examples include:

1. Technical Skills: Depending on the industry and function of the team, technical skills such as proficiency in programming languages, data analysis tools, or project management software may be required.

2. Domain Knowledge: A deep understanding of the relevant industry or domain is often crucial for making informed decisions and driving innovation within the team.

3. Creativity and Innovation: Teams benefit from members who can think outside the box, generate novel ideas, and contribute to creative problem-solving processes.

4. Time Management: Effective time management skills are essential for meeting deadlines, prioritizing tasks, and maximizing productivity.

5. Customer Focus: For teams that directly interact with customers, having a customer-centric mindset and the ability to anticipate and fulfill customer needs is indispensable.

Assessment Methods

Once the key competencies and skills have been identified for a role, the next step is to assess potential candidates to ensure they possess these attributes. Various assessment methods can be utilized, including:

1. Behavioral Interviews: Conducting structured interviews that focus on past experiences can provide insights into candidates' demonstrated competencies and skills.

2. Role-Play Exercises: Simulating real-world scenarios allows candidates to showcase their problem-solving abilities, communication skills, and teamwork in action.

3. Technical Assessments: For roles that require specific technical skills, administering assessments or coding challenges can help evaluate candidates' proficiency in those areas.

4. Psychometric Tests: Assessments such as personality tests or cognitive ability tests can provide additional information about candidates' personality traits, decision-making styles, and cognitive abilities.

5. Reference Checks: Contacting references provided by the candidates can offer valuable perspectives on their past performance, teamwork skills, and overall fit for the role.

Conclusion

Identifying the key competencies and skills required for building a high-performance team is a foundational step in the process of selecting the right team members. By understanding the role requirements, defining core competencies, identifying role-specific skills, and employing appropriate assessment methods, managers can ensure that they assemble a team capable of achieving excellence and driving success within the organization.

5.2 Conducting Effective Team Member Recruitment

Recruitment is the cornerstone of building a high-performing team. A successful recruitment process ensures that you attract candidates who not only possess the necessary skills and competencies but also align with your team's culture and values. In this section, we will delve into the strategies and best practices for conducting effective team member recruitment.

Understanding Your Team's Needs

Before embarking on the recruitment process, it's crucial to have a clear understanding of your team's needs. This involves identifying the specific skills, competencies, and qualities required for success in the role. Start by conducting a thorough job analysis, which entails breaking down the job responsibilities, required qualifications, and desired attributes. Engage with key stakeholders, including team members and department heads, to gain insights into the role's requirements.

Crafting Compelling Job Descriptions

A well-crafted job description serves as the first point of contact between your organization and potential candidates. It should provide a comprehensive overview of the role, including responsibilities, qualifications, and expectations. Here are some key elements to include:

- *Job Title and Summary:* Clearly state the title of the position and provide a brief summary of the role's purpose and primary objectives.

- *Key Responsibilities:* Outline the main duties and responsibilities associated with the role, focusing on both day-to-day tasks and long-term objectives.

- *Required Qualifications:* Specify the essential qualifications, such as education, certifications, and years of experience, necessary for the role.

- *Desired Skills and Attributes:* Highlight any additional skills, competencies, or personal qualities that would contribute to success in the role.

- *Company Overview:* Provide an overview of your organization, including its mission, values, and culture, to help candidates gauge their fit.

Utilizing Multiple Recruitment Channels

To reach a diverse pool of qualified candidates, it's essential to leverage a variety of recruitment channels. These may include:

- *Online Job Boards:* Post your job openings on popular job boards and professional networking sites to attract active job seekers.

- *Social Media Platforms:* Utilize social media platforms such as LinkedIn, Twitter, and Facebook to promote job opportunities and engage with potential candidates.

- *Employee Referrals:* Encourage your existing employees to refer qualified candidates from their networks. Employee referrals often result in higher-quality hires and contribute to a strong team culture.

- *Networking Events:* Attend industry conferences, career fairs, and networking events to connect with potential candidates and build relationships within the professional community.

- *Recruitment Agencies:* Partner with reputable recruitment agencies or headhunters specializing in your industry to access their talent pools and expertise in candidate sourcing.

Implementing a Structured Interview Process

Interviews play a pivotal role in assessing candidates' suitability for the role and evaluating their fit within the team. To ensure consistency and fairness, establish a structured interview process that includes the following steps:

- *Pre-Screening:* Conduct initial screenings, such as phone interviews or online assessments, to evaluate candidates' basic qualifications and interest in the role.

- *Behavioral Interviews:* Use behavioral interview techniques to assess candidates' past experiences, behaviors, and problem-solving abilities. Ask open-ended questions that prompt candidates to provide specific examples of their skills and accomplishments.

- *Technical Assessments:* For roles requiring specific technical skills or expertise, administer technical assessments or practical exercises to evaluate candidates' proficiency.

- *Panel Interviews:* Involving multiple team members or stakeholders in the interview process allows for diverse perspectives and helps assess cultural fit.

- *Reference Checks:* Contact the candidate's references to verify their employment history, performance, and character.

Emphasizing Diversity and Inclusion

Diversity and inclusion should be central considerations throughout the recruitment process. Aim to attract candidates from diverse backgrounds and experiences to foster innovation, creativity, and perspective within your team. Implement strategies to mitigate bias and promote equity, such as:

- *Diverse Interview Panels:* Ensure that interview panels represent a diverse range of perspectives, backgrounds, and identities.

- *Unbiased Job Advertisements:* Use inclusive language and imagery in job postings to appeal to a broad audience and avoid unintentional bias.

- *Implicit Bias Training:* Provide training to hiring managers and interviewers on identifying and mitigating unconscious bias in the recruitment process.

- *Diverse Candidate Sourcing:* Actively seek out candidates from underrepresented groups through targeted outreach and partnerships with diversity-focused organizations.

Communicating Transparently with Candidates

Effective communication is essential throughout the recruitment process to keep candidates informed and engaged. Provide timely updates on the status of their application, next steps in the process, and any relevant information about the role or organization. Transparency builds trust and helps create a positive candidate experience, regardless of the outcome.

Conclusion

Conducting effective team member recruitment requires careful planning, strategic execution, and a commitment to diversity and inclusion. By understanding your team's needs, crafting compelling job descriptions, leveraging multiple recruitment channels, implementing a structured interview process, emphasizing diversity and inclusion, and communicating transparently with candidates, you can attract top talent and build a high-performing team poised for success.

5.3 Ensuring Diversity and Inclusion in Team Composition

In today's dynamic and multicultural workplace, diversity and inclusion have become not just buzzwords but essential components of building high-performance teams. A diverse team brings together individuals from different backgrounds, cultures, perspectives, and experiences, which can lead to enhanced creativity, innovation, and problem-solving abilities. However, ensuring diversity and inclusion in team composition goes beyond merely assembling a group of people with different demographics. It requires a deliberate and proactive approach from managers and team leaders to create an environment where every team member feels valued, respected, and empowered to contribute their best. In this section, we will explore strategies for promoting diversity and inclusion within your team.

Understanding Diversity and Inclusion

Before diving into strategies, it's crucial to understand what diversity and inclusion mean in the context of team composition. Diversity encompasses visible attributes such as race, gender, age, ethnicity, sexual orientation, and physical abilities, as well as less visible characteristics like educational background, socioeconomic status, and cognitive styles. Inclusion, on the other hand, refers to the extent to which every individual feels welcomed, respected, and valued for who they are, regardless of their differences.

The Business Case for Diversity and Inclusion

Numerous studies have shown that diverse teams outperform homogeneous ones in various aspects. McKinsey's research, for instance, found that companies with gender-diverse executive teams were 21% more likely to experience above-average profitability. Similarly, organizations with ethnically diverse teams were 33% more likely to outperform their peers in terms of financial performance. These findings underscore the business case for diversity and inclusion, indicating that they are not just moral imperatives but also strategic advantages.

Strategies for Promoting Diversity and Inclusion

1. Establish a Culture of Inclusion

Creating a culture of inclusion starts with leadership commitment. Leaders must actively champion diversity and inclusion initiatives and communicate their importance throughout the organization. They should set clear expectations for behavior and hold everyone accountable for fostering an inclusive environment. Regular training sessions on unconscious bias, cultural competence, and inclusive leadership can help raise awareness and cultivate inclusive behaviors among team members.

2. Foster Psychological Safety

Psychological safety is essential for ensuring that all team members feel comfortable expressing their ideas, opinions, and concerns without fear of judgment or reprisal. Leaders can promote psychological safety by encouraging open communication, actively listening to diverse perspectives, and valuing dissenting opinions. Team-building activities, such as icebreaker exercises and group discussions, can also help strengthen trust and cohesion within the team.

3. Implement Bias-Free Recruitment Practices

To ensure a diverse talent pipeline, it's crucial to implement bias-free recruitment practices at every stage of the hiring process. This includes using diverse job boards and recruitment channels, crafting inclusive job descriptions, and employing structured interviews with standardized questions. Additionally, blind resume screening can help mitigate unconscious bias by removing identifying information such as names, genders, and photos from applicants' resumes.

4. Embrace Diversity in Decision-Making

Diverse teams are more effective when it comes to problem-solving and decision-making, as they bring a wider range of perspectives and insights to the table. Leaders should embrace diversity in decision-making by soliciting input from all team members, regardless of their seniority or background. Creating opportunities for collaborative decision-making, such as brainstorming sessions and group discussions, can foster creativity and innovation within the team.

5. Provide Diversity Training and Education

Continuous education and training are essential for building cultural competence and promoting diversity awareness within the team. Leaders should provide regular diversity training sessions covering topics such as unconscious bias, cultural sensitivity, and inclusive communication. These sessions can help team members recognize and challenge their own biases, foster empathy and understanding across differences, and promote respectful and inclusive interactions.

6. Celebrate Diversity and Achievements

Acknowledging and celebrating diversity within the team can help foster a sense of belonging and inclusion among team members. Leaders should recognize and appreciate the unique contributions and perspectives that each individual brings to the team. This can be done through employee spotlights, diversity awards, and cultural celebrations that highlight different holidays, traditions, and customs. By celebrating diversity, teams can cultivate a positive and inclusive work environment where everyone feels valued and respected.

Conclusion

In today's globalized and interconnected world, diversity and inclusion are no longer optional but imperative for building high-performance teams. By embracing diversity and creating an inclusive work environment, organizations can unlock the full potential of their teams, drive innovation and creativity, and achieve sustainable success in the long run. As a manager or team leader, it's essential to take proactive steps to promote diversity and inclusion within your team, from establishing a culture of inclusion to implementing bias-free recruitment practices and providing ongoing diversity training and education. By doing so, you can create a team where every individual feels valued, respected, and empowered to contribute their unique talents and perspectives towards shared goals and objectives.

6. Fostering Team Collaboration and Trust

6.1 Creating a Culture of Open Communication

In the modern workplace, fostering a culture of open communication is not just a desirable trait; it's a necessity for building high-performance teams. Open communication lays the foundation for trust, transparency, and collaboration within a team. It enables team members to express their ideas, concerns, and feedback freely, fostering a sense of belonging and empowerment. This chapter delves into the strategies and practices managers can employ to cultivate a culture of open communication within their teams.

Understanding the Importance of Open Communication

Open communication is more than just exchanging information; it's about creating an environment where every team member feels comfortable sharing their thoughts, opinions, and feelings without fear of judgment or reprisal. When team members communicate openly, it leads to increased clarity, alignment, and innovation. Moreover, open communication fosters a sense of psychological safety, where individuals feel valued and respected, leading to higher levels of engagement and productivity.

Key Components of Open Communication

To cultivate a culture of open communication, managers must focus on several key components:

1. Active Listening: Encourage team members to actively listen to one another without interrupting or judging. Active listening involves paying full attention to what the other person is saying, empathizing with their perspective, and responding thoughtfully.

2. Transparency: Be transparent about the organization's goals, strategies, and challenges. Share information openly with your team members, including both successes and failures. Transparency builds trust and fosters a sense of shared purpose.

3. Encouraging Feedback: Create channels for providing and receiving feedback regularly. Feedback should be constructive, specific, and focused on behaviors or actions rather than personal attributes. Encourage a culture where feedback is seen as an opportunity for growth and improvement.

4. Empowering Voice: Ensure that every team member feels empowered to voice their opinions and ideas. Avoid dominating discussions or dismissing dissenting viewpoints. Encourage diverse perspectives and foster an inclusive environment where everyone feels valued.

5. Respectful Communication: Emphasize the importance of respectful communication within the team. Set clear guidelines for communication, including language, tone, and demeanor. Address any conflicts or disrespectful behavior promptly to maintain a positive team culture.

Strategies for Cultivating Open Communication

Building a culture of open communication requires deliberate effort and consistent reinforcement. Here are some strategies that managers can employ:

1. Lead by Example: As a manager, demonstrate open communication in your interactions with your team members. Model active listening, transparency, and receptivity to feedback. Your behavior sets the tone for the team's communication culture.

2. Establish Regular Check-ins: Schedule regular one-on-one meetings with each team member to discuss their progress, challenges, and goals. Use these meetings as opportunities to listen actively, provide feedback, and address any concerns they may have.

3. Create Forums for Discussion: Organize team meetings, brainstorming sessions, or workshops where team members can openly share their ideas, experiences, and perspectives. Create a safe space where everyone feels encouraged to contribute without fear of judgment.

4. Utilize Technology: Leverage technology tools such as communication platforms, project management software, or anonymous feedback systems to facilitate communication within the team. Choose tools that are user-friendly and align with the team's preferences and needs.

5. Encourage Social Interaction: Foster opportunities for informal social interaction among team members, such as team lunches, coffee breaks, or virtual hangouts. Building personal connections outside of work-related tasks strengthens trust and rapport within the team.

6. Provide Communication Training: Offer training or workshops on effective communication skills, including active listening, conflict resolution, and giving/receiving feedback. Equip team members with the tools they need to communicate confidently and respectfully.

Overcoming Challenges

While fostering open communication is essential, it can also present challenges that managers need to address:

1. Overcoming Resistance: Some team members may be hesitant to communicate openly due to past negative experiences or fear of repercussions. Managers should address these concerns empathetically and create a supportive environment where everyone feels valued and heard.

2. Managing Conflicts: Open communication can sometimes lead to conflicts or disagreements within the team. Managers should be prepared to mediate conflicts constructively, focusing on finding mutually beneficial solutions and preserving relationships.

3. Balancing Transparency: While transparency is important, there may be sensitive information that cannot be shared openly with the entire team. Managers need to strike a balance between transparency and confidentiality, being honest about what can be shared while respecting privacy and organizational boundaries.

Conclusion

In conclusion, creating a culture of open communication is fundamental to building high-performance teams. By prioritizing active listening, transparency, feedback, empowerment, and respect, managers can foster an environment where team members feel valued, heard, and motivated to contribute their best. Cultivating open communication requires ongoing commitment and effort, but the rewards in terms of trust, collaboration, and innovation are well worth it. As a manager, investing in open communication is not just a strategy; it's a cornerstone of effective leadership and team success.

6.2 Building Trust and Psychological Safety

Building trust and fostering psychological safety within a team are foundational elements for high performance and innovation. Trust is the cornerstone of any successful relationship, whether personal or professional, and without it, collaboration and productivity can suffer. Similarly, psychological safety is crucial for team members to feel comfortable taking risks, expressing their ideas, and challenging the status quo without fear of reprisal or judgment. In this section, we delve into strategies and practices that managers can employ to cultivate trust and psychological safety within their teams.

Understanding Trust

Trust is a multifaceted concept that encompasses reliability, integrity, competence, and benevolence. It is built over time through consistent actions, transparency, and open communication. Trust within a team enables individuals to rely on one another, share information freely, and collaborate effectively. Without trust, team members may hesitate to ask for help, share their opinions, or admit their mistakes, which can hinder the team's progress and erode morale.

1. Lead by Example

Managers play a pivotal role in establishing trust within their teams. Leaders who demonstrate integrity, transparency, and reliability set the tone for trustworthiness. They uphold their commitments, communicate openly and honestly, and admit their own fallibility. By modeling these behaviors, managers encourage their team members to do the same, creating a culture of trust from the top down.

2. Encourage Vulnerability

Vulnerability is often viewed as a weakness, but in reality, it is a strength that fosters connection and trust. Encouraging team members to share their challenges, failures, and insecurities creates a sense of camaraderie and empathy. When individuals feel safe enough to be vulnerable, they are more likely to trust one another and collaborate more effectively. Managers can facilitate vulnerability by sharing their own struggles and demonstrating empathy towards their team members.

3. Provide Constructive Feedback

Feedback is essential for growth and development, but it must be delivered in a way that is constructive and supportive. Managers should strive to provide feedback that is specific, timely, and actionable, focusing on behaviors rather than personalities. By offering praise for accomplishments and constructive criticism for areas of improvement, managers can help their team members learn and grow without feeling threatened or discouraged.

4. Foster Inclusivity

Inclusive teams are built on trust and respect for diversity. Managers should actively promote inclusivity by valuing diverse perspectives, creating opportunities for all team members to contribute, and addressing any instances of bias or discrimination. By fostering a culture of inclusivity, managers can ensure that every team member feels valued, respected, and empowered to fully participate in team activities.

Understanding Psychological Safety

Psychological safety is the belief that one will not be punished or humiliated for speaking up with ideas, questions, concerns, or mistakes. It is a fundamental aspect of team dynamics that enables individuals to take interpersonal risks without fear of negative consequences. Teams with high levels of psychological safety are more likely to engage in candid discussions, experiment with new ideas, and learn from failure, leading to greater innovation and performance.

1. Foster Open Communication

Effective communication is essential for creating psychological safety within a team. Managers should encourage open dialogue, active listening, and constructive feedback. Team members should feel comfortable expressing their thoughts, opinions, and concerns without fear of judgment or reprisal. By fostering a culture of open communication, managers can ensure that all voices are heard and respected.

2. Embrace Failure as a Learning Opportunity

Failure is inevitable in any creative endeavor, but it is how teams respond to failure that determines their success. Managers should encourage a growth mindset, where failure is seen as a natural part of the learning process rather than a source of shame or blame. By reframing failure as a learning opportunity, managers can help their team members take risks, experiment with new ideas, and ultimately innovate more effectively.

3. Encourage Collaboration and Teamwork

Collaboration is essential for fostering psychological safety within a team. When team members collaborate effectively, they feel supported and valued by their peers, which enhances their sense of belonging and reduces feelings of isolation or inadequacy. Managers should encourage collaboration through team-building activities, shared goals, and collaborative projects that allow team members to leverage each other's strengths and expertise.

4. Lead with Empathy

Empathy is the ability to understand and share the feelings of others, and it is a critical component of psychological safety. Managers should demonstrate empathy towards their team members by actively listening to their concerns, acknowledging their emotions, and providing support and encouragement when needed. By leading with empathy, managers can create a supportive and compassionate work environment where team members feel understood and valued.

Conclusion

Building trust and fostering psychological safety within a team are ongoing processes that require intentionality, effort, and commitment from both managers and team members. By prioritizing open communication, vulnerability, inclusivity, and empathy, managers can create a culture where trust flourishes, and individuals feel safe to take risks, share their ideas, and collaborate effectively. Ultimately, teams that prioritize trust and psychological safety are better equipped to navigate challenges, drive innovation, and achieve success together.

6.3 Promoting Collaboration and Teamwork

Promoting collaboration and teamwork within a team is essential for achieving high performance and success in any organization. When team members work together effectively, they can leverage their collective strengths, skills, and knowledge to accomplish shared goals and objectives. In this section, we will explore strategies and practices that managers can implement to promote collaboration and teamwork within their teams.

1. Establish Clear Goals and Expectations

One of the first steps in promoting collaboration and teamwork is to establish clear goals and expectations for the team. When team members have a clear understanding of what they are working towards, they can align their efforts and collaborate more effectively. Managers should communicate the team's goals and objectives clearly and ensure that each team member understands their role in achieving them. Additionally, setting clear expectations for collaboration, communication, and accountability can help create a framework for teamwork.

2. Encourage Open Communication

Open communication is the foundation of collaboration and teamwork. Managers should create an environment where team members feel comfortable sharing their ideas, concerns, and feedback openly. Encouraging open communication can help foster trust among team members and promote a culture of transparency and collaboration. Managers can facilitate open communication by organizing regular team meetings, providing opportunities for team members to voice their opinions, and actively listening to their input.

3. Foster a Culture of Collaboration

Building a culture of collaboration requires more than just encouraging teamwork; it involves creating an environment where collaboration is valued and rewarded. Managers can foster a culture of collaboration by recognizing and celebrating team achievements, promoting cross-functional collaboration, and providing resources and support for collaborative projects. Additionally, managers should lead by example by actively collaborating with team members and demonstrating the benefits of working together towards common goals.

4. Establish Clear Roles and Responsibilities

Clarity around roles and responsibilities is essential for effective collaboration. When team members understand their roles and how they contribute to the team's success, they can work together more efficiently. Managers should take the time to define each team member's role and responsibilities clearly, ensuring that there is no confusion or overlap. Additionally, managers should encourage team members to collaborate and support each other by leveraging their individual strengths and expertise.

5. Promote Diversity and Inclusion

Diversity and inclusion are critical components of effective collaboration and teamwork. When teams are composed of individuals from diverse backgrounds, experiences, and perspectives, they can bring unique insights and ideas to the table. Managers should promote diversity and inclusion within their teams by fostering an inclusive environment where all team members feel valued and respected. This may involve implementing diversity training programs, addressing unconscious bias, and creating opportunities for diverse voices to be heard.

6. Provide Opportunities for Skill Development

Investing in skill development is essential for building a high-performing team. Managers should provide opportunities for team members to develop their skills and expand their knowledge through training, workshops, and mentorship programs. By investing in their development, managers can empower team members to take on new challenges and contribute more effectively to collaborative projects. Additionally, providing opportunities for skill development can help build trust and camaraderie among team members as they learn and grow together.

7. Encourage Flexibility and Adaptability

In today's fast-paced business environment, flexibility and adaptability are key to successful collaboration. Managers should encourage team members to be open to new ideas, embrace change, and adapt to evolving circumstances. This may involve being willing to pivot or adjust project plans as needed and encouraging a mindset of continuous improvement. By fostering flexibility and adaptability within the team, managers can ensure that their teams are well-equipped to collaborate effectively and respond to challenges as they arise.

8. Facilitate Team-Building Activities

Team-building activities can be a valuable tool for promoting collaboration and teamwork. Whether it's participating in outdoor challenges, volunteering together, or simply socializing outside of work, team-building activities can help strengthen bonds among team members and foster a sense of camaraderie. Managers should organize regular team-building activities to provide opportunities for team members to connect on a personal level and build trust and rapport with one another.

Conclusion

Promoting collaboration and teamwork within a team is essential for achieving high performance and success. By establishing clear goals and expectations, encouraging open communication, fostering a culture of collaboration, and providing opportunities for skill development, managers can create an environment where team members can work together effectively towards shared goals. Additionally, promoting diversity and inclusion, encouraging flexibility and adaptability, and facilitating team-building activities can help strengthen bonds among team members and enhance collaboration. By implementing these strategies and practices, managers can build and develop high-performing teams that are capable of achieving extraordinary results.

Example: Project X - Fostering Team Collaboration and Trust

Background:

John is a project manager leading a team of software developers at a technology company. The team is responsible for developing a new mobile application called "Project X," which aims to revolutionize the way users manage their daily tasks and schedules.

1. Establish Clear Goals and Expectations:

At the beginning of the Project X development process, John gathers his team for a kickoff meeting. During the meeting, he clearly articulates the project's goals, timeline, and key deliverables. He ensures that each team member understands their role in the project and what is expected of them. John emphasizes the importance of collaboration and teamwork in achieving the project's objectives.

2. Encourage Open Communication:

John creates an open and inclusive environment where team members feel comfortable sharing their ideas, concerns, and feedback. He schedules regular team meetings where team members have the opportunity to discuss their progress, challenges, and ideas openly. John actively listens to his team members' input and encourages them to voice their opinions without fear of judgment.

3. Foster a Culture of Collaboration:

To foster a culture of collaboration, John promotes cross-functional collaboration within his team. He encourages team members to work together across different departments and disciplines to leverage their diverse skills and expertise. John organizes brainstorming sessions and collaborative workshops where team members can collaborate on solving complex problems and generating innovative ideas.

4. Establish Clear Roles and Responsibilities:

John ensures that each team member understands their role and responsibilities within the project. He creates a project charter outlining the roles and responsibilities of each team member, as well as the project's overall objectives and scope. John emphasizes the importance of teamwork and encourages team members to support each other in achieving their goals.

5. Promote Diversity and Inclusion:

Recognizing the value of diversity and inclusion, John actively promotes diversity within his team. He encourages team members from different backgrounds, experiences, and perspectives to contribute their unique insights and ideas to the project. John ensures that all team members feel valued and respected, regardless of their gender, race, or background.

6. Provide Opportunities for Skill Development:

John invests in his team members' skill development by providing opportunities for training, workshops, and mentorship programs. He identifies areas where team members can improve their skills and offers resources and support to help them succeed. John encourages team members to take on new challenges and expand their knowledge to enhance their contributions to the project.

7. Encourage Flexibility and Adaptability:

In the dynamic world of software development, John understands the importance of flexibility and adaptability. He encourages his team members to be open to new ideas, embrace change, and adapt to evolving circumstances. John leads by example by being flexible in his approach to project management and encouraging his team to be agile in their problem-solving.

8. Facilitate Team-Building Activities:

To strengthen bonds among team members and foster trust and camaraderie, John organizes regular team-building activities. These activities range from team lunches and happy hours to outdoor team-building exercises and volunteer opportunities. Through these activities, team members have the chance to connect on a personal level and build lasting relationships outside of work.

Conclusion:

Through John's leadership and commitment to fostering collaboration and trust, the Project X team successfully develops the mobile application on time and within budget. By establishing clear goals and expectations, encouraging open communication, fostering a culture of collaboration, and providing opportunities for skill development, John creates an environment where team members can thrive and achieve extraordinary results together.

7. Providing Effective Team Training and Development

7.1 Assessing Team Training Needs

Assessing team training needs is a critical step in ensuring the effectiveness and efficiency of a team. It involves identifying the skills, knowledge, and competencies required for team members to perform their roles effectively and achieve team goals. By conducting a thorough assessment, managers can tailor training programs to address specific gaps and enhance the overall performance of the team. This section explores various methods and strategies for assessing team training needs.

Understanding the Importance of Assessing Training Needs

Before delving into the assessment methods, it's essential to understand why assessing training needs is crucial for team development. Here are some key reasons:

1. Identifying Skill Gaps: Assessing training needs helps identify gaps between the current skills and knowledge of team members and the skills required to perform their roles effectively. This allows managers to focus resources on areas where improvement is most needed.

2. Improving Performance: Targeted training programs can help improve the performance of individual team members and the team as a whole. By addressing specific skill deficiencies, teams can work more efficiently and achieve better results.

3. Enhancing Employee Engagement: Providing opportunities for training and development demonstrates a commitment to employees' growth and career advancement. This can lead to increased job satisfaction, motivation, and engagement within the team.

4. Staying Competitive: In today's fast-paced business environment, staying ahead of the competition requires continuous learning and skill development. Assessing training needs ensures that teams have the necessary capabilities to adapt to changing market conditions and technological advancements.

Methods for Assessing Team Training Needs

There are several methods and approaches managers can use to assess team training needs. The most effective approach will depend on factors such as the size and structure of the team, the nature of the work, and the available resources. Here are some common methods:

1. Skill Gap Analysis: Conducting a skill gap analysis involves comparing the skills and competencies required for each team member's role with their current skill levels. This can be done through self-assessment, manager assessments, or competency-based evaluations. The gaps identified can then be addressed through targeted training programs.

2. Performance Reviews: Performance reviews provide valuable insights into the strengths and weaknesses of individual team members. Managers can use performance data, feedback from peers and supervisors, and self-assessments to identify areas where additional training or development is needed.

3. Surveys and Questionnaires: Surveys and questionnaires can be used to gather feedback from team members about their training needs, preferences, and challenges. This can help identify common themes and areas of consensus, which can inform the design of training programs.

4. Observation and Job Analysis: Observing team members in their work environment and conducting job analyses can provide valuable information about the specific tasks, skills, and knowledge required for each role. This can help identify areas where training or development is needed to improve performance.

5. Industry Benchmarking: Benchmarking against industry standards and best practices can help identify areas where the team may be lagging behind or where there are opportunities for improvement. This can inform the selection of training programs and initiatives to bridge the gap.

6. Future Skills Analysis: Anticipating future trends and changes in the industry can help identify emerging skills and competencies that will be critical for the team's success. Managers can then proactively develop training programs to equip team members with these future-oriented skills.

Designing a Training Needs Assessment Process

To effectively assess team training needs, managers should follow a structured process that includes the following steps:

1. Define Objectives: Clarify the objectives of the training needs assessment, including the desired outcomes and how the assessment will support the team's goals and objectives.

2. Gather Data: Collect data from various sources, including performance reviews, surveys, observation, and industry benchmarks. Ensure that the data gathered is relevant, accurate, and comprehensive.

3. Analyze Data: Analyze the data to identify patterns, trends, and areas of concern. Look for common themes and prioritize training needs based on their impact on team performance and goals.

4. Engage Stakeholders: Involve key stakeholders, including team members, supervisors, HR professionals, and subject matter experts, in the assessment process. Seek their input and feedback to ensure buy-in and support for the training initiatives.

5. Develop Action Plan: Based on the findings of the assessment, develop a detailed action plan that outlines the specific training programs, resources, and timelines needed to address the identified gaps.

6. Implement Training Programs: Implement the training programs according to the action plan, ensuring that they are tailored to meet the needs of individual team members and the team as a whole.

7. Monitor and Evaluate: Continuously monitor and evaluate the effectiveness of the training programs, soliciting feedback from participants and tracking key performance indicators. Make adjustments as needed to ensure that the training initiatives are achieving the desired results.

By following these steps, managers can effectively assess team training needs and develop targeted training programs that enhance the capabilities and performance of their teams. Investing in training and development not only benefits individual team members but also contributes to the overall success and competitiveness of the organization.

7.2 Designing Tailored Training Programs

Designing tailored training programs is a crucial aspect of building high-performance teams. While generic training modules have their merits, they often fall short in addressing the specific needs and challenges of individual teams. Tailored training programs, on the other hand, are crafted to align with the unique dynamics, goals, and skill gaps of a particular team. In this section, we delve into the key steps involved in designing such programs and explore various strategies to maximize their effectiveness.

Understanding Team Dynamics and Needs

Before embarking on the design of a tailored training program, it's essential to gain a comprehensive understanding of the team's dynamics and specific training needs. This involves conducting thorough assessments, gathering feedback from team members, and analyzing performance data. By identifying areas of strength and weakness, managers can pinpoint the skills and competencies that require enhancement.

One effective approach is to use diagnostic tools such as surveys, interviews, and performance evaluations to assess the current state of the team. These tools can provide valuable insights into factors such as communication patterns, collaboration effectiveness, and individual skill levels. Additionally, soliciting input directly from team members fosters a sense of ownership and engagement in the training process.

Setting Clear Objectives

With a solid understanding of the team's needs, the next step is to establish clear training objectives. These objectives should be specific, measurable, achievable, relevant, and time-bound (SMART) to ensure clarity and focus. By articulating clear goals, managers can effectively communicate the intended outcomes of the training program and align them with the team's overall mission and objectives.

For example, if the team is struggling with project management skills, the training objective could be to improve project planning and execution processes, leading to more efficient project delivery and higher client satisfaction. By setting specific targets, such as reducing project timelines by 20% within six months, managers provide a clear benchmark for success and motivate team members to actively participate in the training program.

Customizing Content and Delivery Methods

One of the key advantages of tailored training programs is the ability to customize content and delivery methods to suit the unique needs and preferences of the team. Instead of relying on off-the-shelf training materials, managers can collaborate with subject matter experts to develop customized content that addresses the specific challenges faced by the team.

This may involve incorporating real-life case studies, simulations, and role-playing exercises that are directly relevant to the team's context. For example, if the team operates in a highly regulated industry such as healthcare or finance, training modules could focus on compliance requirements, risk management strategies, and ethical decision-making processes.

In addition to customizing content, managers should also consider the most effective delivery methods for the training program. While traditional classroom-style training sessions have their place, they may not always be the most engaging or practical option, especially for busy teams with demanding schedules.

Alternative delivery methods such as online courses, webinars, microlearning modules, and on-the-job training sessions offer greater flexibility and convenience. By leveraging a blend of different delivery methods, managers can accommodate diverse learning styles and preferences within the team while ensuring maximum accessibility and engagement.

Fostering Active Participation and Engagement

One of the biggest challenges in designing training programs is ensuring active participation and engagement from team members. To overcome this challenge, managers must create a supportive and inclusive learning environment that encourages participation and collaboration.

One effective strategy is to incorporate interactive elements such as group discussions, team exercises, and peer-to-peer learning activities into the training program. These activities not only reinforce key concepts but also provide opportunities for team members to share insights, learn from each other's experiences, and build stronger bonds.

Additionally, managers should actively seek feedback from participants throughout the training program to gauge effectiveness and identify areas for improvement. By soliciting input on topics, delivery methods, and overall satisfaction, managers demonstrate their commitment to continuous improvement and create a culture of open communication and feedback within the team.

Measuring and Evaluating Impact

Finally, it's essential to measure and evaluate the impact of the training program to determine its effectiveness and return on investment. This involves tracking key performance metrics before, during, and after the training intervention to assess changes in behavior, skills, and performance.

Some common metrics for evaluating training impact include:

- Knowledge acquisition: Assessing the extent to which participants have acquired new knowledge and skills as a result of the training program.

- Behavior change: Observing changes in behavior, attitudes, and practices among team members following the training intervention.

- Performance improvement: Measuring improvements in key performance indicators such as productivity, quality, and customer satisfaction.

- Return on investment (ROI): Calculating the financial benefits generated by the training program relative to the costs incurred, taking into account factors such as increased revenue, cost savings, and productivity gains.

By collecting and analyzing relevant data, managers can gain valuable insights into the effectiveness of the training program and make informed decisions about future training initiatives.

Conclusion

Designing tailored training programs is essential for building high-performance teams that are equipped with the skills and competencies needed to succeed in today's dynamic business environment. By understanding team dynamics, setting clear objectives, customizing content and delivery methods, fostering active participation and engagement, and measuring impact, managers can create training programs that deliver tangible results and drive continuous improvement. With a strategic approach to training and development, organizations can empower their teams to reach their full potential and achieve sustainable success.

7.3 Implementing Continuous Learning Initiatives

Implementing continuous learning initiatives within your team is crucial for maintaining competitiveness, adapting to change, and fostering a culture of growth and improvement. In today's fast-paced work environment, where technological advancements and market dynamics evolve rapidly, embracing a mindset of lifelong learning is essential. This section explores strategies and best practices for effectively implementing continuous learning initiatives within your team.

1. Establishing a Learning Culture

Creating a culture that values and prioritizes learning is the foundation of successful continuous learning initiatives. Leaders play a pivotal role in setting the tone and demonstrating commitment to ongoing development. Here are key steps to establish a learning culture:

- *Lead by Example:* Managers and team leaders should actively engage in learning activities and demonstrate the importance of continuous improvement.

- *Communicate Expectations:* Clearly communicate to team members that continuous learning is not only encouraged but expected as part of their professional development.

- *Recognize and Reward Learning:* Acknowledge and reward individuals and teams who actively pursue learning opportunities and apply new knowledge and skills to their work.

- *Provide Resources:* Ensure access to resources such as training programs, online courses, workshops, and learning materials to support employees' learning journey.

- *Encourage Collaboration:* Foster a collaborative environment where team members can share knowledge, insights, and experiences with each other.

2. Tailoring Learning Initiatives

One size does not fit all when it comes to learning initiatives. Recognize that each team member has unique learning preferences, goals, and developmental needs. Tailoring learning initiatives ensures relevance and maximizes engagement. Here's how to customize learning experiences:

- *Conduct Learning Needs Assessments:* Regularly assess the learning needs and preferences of individual team members and the team as a whole. This can be done through surveys, one-on-one discussions, performance evaluations, and feedback sessions.

- *Offer Diverse Learning Opportunities*: Provide a variety of learning options to accommodate different learning styles and preferences. This may include instructor-led training, online courses, workshops, seminars, peer-to-peer learning, and self-paced learning modules.

- *Align with Career Goals:* Link learning initiatives with employees' career aspirations and development plans. Help them identify relevant skills and knowledge areas that align with their long-term goals.

- *Provide Flexibility*: Offer flexible learning options that allow employees to balance learning activities with their daily responsibilities. This could involve scheduling dedicated learning time, providing access to online resources, or supporting attendance at relevant events and conferences.

3. Leveraging Technology

Technology plays a pivotal role in facilitating continuous learning initiatives by providing access to a wealth of learning resources and tools. Leverage technology to create immersive and engaging learning experiences. Here are ways to harness technology for continuous learning:

- *Online Learning Platforms:* Invest in learning management systems (LMS) or subscribe to online learning platforms that offer a diverse range of courses and resources. These platforms often feature interactive content, assessments, and progress tracking capabilities.

- *Microlearning:* Embrace microlearning techniques, which deliver content in short, digestible bursts. This approach is well-suited for busy schedules and enables learners to consume information in smaller increments.

- *Virtual Reality (VR) and Augmented Reality (AR)*: Explore the potential of VR and AR technologies to create immersive learning experiences. These technologies simulate real-world scenarios and environments, allowing learners to practice skills in a safe and controlled setting.

- *Gamification:* Incorporate gamification elements into learning initiatives to enhance engagement and motivation. This could involve awarding badges, points, or levels for completing learning tasks and achieving milestones.

4. Fostering Continuous Feedback and Reflection

Feedback and reflection are integral components of the learning process. Encourage a culture of continuous feedback and reflection to facilitate ongoing improvement. Here's how to promote feedback and reflection:

- *Regular Check-Ins:* Schedule regular check-in meetings or performance reviews to discuss progress, challenges, and learning goals. Provide constructive feedback and guidance to help employees address areas for improvement.

- *Peer Coaching and Mentoring:* Encourage peer coaching and mentoring relationships within the team. Pair experienced team members with those seeking guidance and support in specific skill areas or projects.

- *Encourage Self-Reflection:* Encourage employees to reflect on their learning experiences, successes, and areas for growth. This could be done through journaling, self-assessments, or facilitated reflection sessions.

- *Celebrate Progress:* Celebrate achievements and milestones along the learning journey. Recognize and reward individuals and teams for their dedication to continuous improvement.

5. Measuring Learning Impact

Effectively measuring the impact of learning initiatives is essential for evaluating their effectiveness and informing future investment decisions. Implement strategies to assess learning outcomes and measure return on investment (ROI). Here are key considerations for measuring learning impact:

- *Define Key Performance Indicators (KPIs):* Identify specific KPIs related to learning objectives, such as knowledge acquisition, skill development, performance improvement, and behavior change.

- *Collect Data:* Gather data through various methods, including pre- and post-training assessments, surveys, performance evaluations, and feedback from supervisors and peers.

- *Track Progress:* Continuously monitor and track individual and team progress towards learning goals. Utilize learning analytics and reporting tools to visualize trends and identify areas for improvement.

- *Gather Feedback:* Solicit feedback from participants to assess the effectiveness of learning initiatives, including content relevance, delivery methods, and overall satisfaction.

- *Evaluate Business Impact:* Assess the impact of learning initiatives on business outcomes, such as increased productivity, efficiency gains, quality improvements, and employee retention.

6. Iterating and Evolving

Continuous learning is an ongoing journey that requires adaptation and evolution over time. Embrace a culture of experimentation and continuous improvement to refine learning initiatives and ensure their relevance and effectiveness. Here's how to iterate and evolve:

- *Gather Insights:* Regularly gather insights and feedback from stakeholders, including employees, managers, and subject matter experts. Use this feedback to identify areas for improvement and innovation.

- *Monitor Trends:* Stay abreast of industry trends, technological advancements, and best practices in learning and development. Leverage emerging technologies and methodologies to enhance learning experiences.

- *Pilot New Initiatives:* Experiment with new learning approaches and technologies through pilot programs or small-scale trials. Evaluate their impact and scalability before scaling them across the organization.

- *Encourage Innovation:* Encourage employees to propose and implement innovative ideas to enhance learning initiatives. Create a culture where experimentation and risk-taking are valued and supported.

Conclusion

Implementing continuous learning initiatives is a strategic imperative for building high-performance teams in today's dynamic business landscape. By fostering a culture of learning, tailoring learning experiences, leveraging technology, promoting feedback and reflection, measuring learning impact, and iterating and evolving over time, managers can empower their teams to thrive and adapt in an ever-changing environment. Embrace the journey of lifelong learning, and reap the rewards of a skilled, engaged, and resilient workforce.

PART III
Leading and Sustaining High-Performance Teams

8. Empowering Team Members through Leadership

8.1 Developing Transformational Leadership Skills

Transformational leadership is a powerful approach that inspires and motivates team members to achieve extraordinary results. Unlike transactional leadership, which focuses on exchanges and rewards, transformational leadership centers on influencing and inspiring followers to exceed their own expectations. In this section, we will delve into the key principles and strategies for developing transformational leadership skills.

Understanding Transformational Leadership

At its core, transformational leadership revolves around four key components: idealized influence, inspirational motivation, intellectual stimulation, and individualized consideration.

1. Idealized Influence: Transformational leaders serve as role models for their team members. They embody the values and principles they wish to instill in others, earning admiration, respect, and trust.

2. Inspirational Motivation: Transformational leaders articulate a compelling vision for the future. They inspire and motivate their team members by communicating a clear and inspiring vision, fostering enthusiasm and commitment to shared goals.

3. Intellectual Stimulation: Transformational leaders encourage creativity and innovation within their teams. They challenge the status quo, stimulate critical thinking, and foster an environment where team members feel empowered to question assumptions and explore new ideas.

4. Individualized Consideration: Transformational leaders demonstrate genuine concern for the well-being and development of each team member. They provide personalized support, coaching, and mentoring to help individuals unlock their full potential.

Developing Transformational Leadership Skills

Becoming a transformational leader requires a combination of self-awareness, empathy, vision, and effective communication. Here are some strategies to develop transformational leadership skills:

1. Self-Reflection and Assessment: Start by reflecting on your own values, beliefs, and leadership style. Assess your strengths and weaknesses as a leader, and identify areas for growth. Seek feedback from peers, mentors, and team members to gain insights into how others perceive your leadership.

2. Articulate a Compelling Vision: Develop a clear and inspiring vision for your team or organization. Communicate this vision in a way that resonates with team members, highlighting the shared values and goals that unite everyone toward a common purpose.

3. Lead by Example: Act as a role model for your team members by embodying the values and behaviors you wish to see in others. Demonstrate integrity, authenticity, and resilience in your actions, earning the trust and respect of your team.

4. Empower Others: Delegate authority and decision-making responsibilities to team members, empowering them to take ownership of their work and contribute meaningfully to the team's success. Provide guidance and support as needed, but allow individuals the autonomy to make decisions and learn from their experiences.

5. Inspire and Motivate: Inspire enthusiasm and commitment among team members by sharing stories of success, acknowledging individual contributions, and celebrating milestones along the way. Encourage a positive and optimistic outlook, even in the face of challenges.

6. Foster Innovation and Learning: Create an environment that encourages creativity, experimentation, and continuous learning. Encourage team members to explore new ideas, challenge assumptions, and embrace failure as an opportunity for growth and improvement.

7. Cultivate Relationships: Take the time to build strong, trusting relationships with your team members. Show genuine interest in their well-being, listen actively to their concerns, and provide support and guidance when needed. Invest in mentoring and coaching relationships to help individuals develop their skills and reach their full potential.

8. Communicate Effectively: Develop strong communication skills to convey your vision, expectations, and feedback clearly and persuasively. Foster open dialogue and encourage feedback from team members, creating a culture of transparency and trust.

Conclusion

Transformational leadership has the power to elevate team performance and foster a culture of innovation, collaboration, and continuous improvement. By developing transformational leadership skills, managers can inspire and empower their team members to achieve extraordinary results and realize their full potential. Through self-reflection, empathy, vision, and effective communication, leaders can cultivate a culture of excellence and drive sustainable success in their organizations.

8.2 Empowering Team Members to Make Decisions

Empowering team members to make decisions is a cornerstone of effective leadership. When team members feel trusted and empowered to make decisions, they become more engaged, motivated, and invested in the success of the team. However, this empowerment does not happen overnight nor is it a one-size-fits-all approach. It requires thoughtful leadership, clear communication, and a supportive environment. In this chapter, we will explore strategies for empowering team members to make decisions and the benefits it brings to the team and organization.

The Importance of Empowering Team Members

Empowering team members to make decisions has numerous benefits for both the team and the organization as a whole. When team members are empowered:

1. Increased Ownership and Accountability: When team members have the authority to make decisions, they take greater ownership of their work and feel a stronger sense of accountability for the outcomes. This leads to higher quality work and greater commitment to achieving team goals.

2. Faster Decision-Making: Empowered team members can make decisions quickly and efficiently, without needing to wait for approval from higher-ups. This agility is essential in today's fast-paced business environment, where quick decision-making can mean the difference between success and failure.

3. Improved Innovation and Creativity: When team members have the freedom to make decisions, they are more likely to think creatively and come up with innovative solutions to challenges. Empowered teams are better able to adapt to change and find new ways to improve processes and achieve objectives.

4. Enhanced Employee Satisfaction and Engagement: Empowered team members feel valued and trusted by their leaders, which leads to higher levels of job satisfaction and engagement. This, in turn, reduces turnover rates and helps attract top talent to the organization.

5. Development of Leadership Skills: Empowering team members to make decisions is a powerful way to develop their leadership skills. By giving them opportunities to take on responsibility and exercise judgment, leaders can help team members grow and develop into future leaders themselves.

Strategies for Empowering Team Members

Empowering team members to make decisions requires a shift in mindset and approach from traditional top-down leadership styles. Here are some strategies leaders can use to empower their teams:

1. Set Clear Expectations: Clearly communicate the goals, objectives, and boundaries within which team members are empowered to make decisions. This helps ensure that everyone is on the same page and understands the scope of their authority.

2. Provide Training and Support: Equip team members with the knowledge, skills, and resources they need to make informed decisions. Offer training programs, mentoring, and coaching to help them develop their decision-making abilities and build confidence in their judgment.

3. Encourage Risk-Taking: Create a culture where taking calculated risks is encouraged and rewarded. Let team members know that it's okay to make mistakes as long as they learn from them and take responsibility for their actions.

4. Delegate Authority: Delegate decision-making authority to team members based on their expertise, experience, and level of responsibility. Trust them to make decisions within their area of competence and only intervene when necessary.

5. Provide Feedback and Recognition: Regularly provide feedback to team members on their decision-making process and outcomes. Recognize and celebrate their successes, and offer constructive criticism when improvements are needed.

6. Lead by Example: Model empowered decision-making behavior yourself as a leader. Demonstrate trust in your team members, seek their input when making decisions, and be transparent about your own decision-making process.

7. Create a Supportive Environment: Foster an environment where team members feel safe to express their opinions, ask questions, and challenge the status quo. Encourage open communication and collaboration, and actively listen to the ideas and concerns of your team members.

Case Study: Empowering Team Members at XYZ Company

To illustrate the benefits of empowering team members to make decisions, let's consider the case of XYZ Company, a software development firm. XYZ Company implemented a strategy to empower its engineering teams to make decisions regarding project planning, resource allocation, and technical solutions. As a result:

- *Increased Productivity:* By empowering engineering teams to make decisions, XYZ Company saw a significant increase in productivity as team members were able to address issues and make changes without waiting for approval from upper management.

- *Improved Employee Morale:* Empowering team members led to higher levels of job satisfaction and morale as employees felt trusted and valued by their leaders. This resulted in lower turnover rates and higher retention of top talent.

- *Faster Time-to-Market:* With empowered teams making decisions, XYZ Company was able to reduce time-to-market for its products, gaining a competitive edge in the industry and increasing revenue.

- *Enhanced Innovation:* Empowered teams at XYZ Company were more innovative and creative in their approach to problem-solving, leading to the development of new features and products that met the evolving needs of customers.

- *Development of Leadership Skills:* Empowering team members provided valuable leadership development opportunities, allowing employees to take on greater responsibility and grow into future leaders within the organization.

Overall, empowering team members to make decisions had a transformative effect on XYZ Company, driving performance improvements and positioning the company for long-term success in the marketplace.

Conclusion

Empowering team members to make decisions is a key aspect of effective leadership and team management. By giving team members the authority and autonomy to make decisions, leaders can unlock their full potential, drive performance improvements, and foster a culture of innovation and collaboration. Through clear communication, training, and support, leaders can empower their teams to take ownership of their work, make informed decisions, and contribute to the success of the organization.

8.3 Supporting and Mentoring Team Members

Supporting and mentoring team members is a crucial aspect of effective leadership within high-performance teams. While empowering team members to make decisions fosters autonomy and ownership, providing support and mentorship ensures that individuals have the resources, guidance, and developmental opportunities needed to thrive. In this section, we will delve into the strategies and best practices for supporting and mentoring team members to enhance their skills, confidence, and overall performance.

The Importance of Support and Mentorship

Support and mentorship play integral roles in shaping the development and success of team members. By offering support, leaders demonstrate their commitment to their team's well-being and growth. Supportive environments encourage open communication, collaboration, and innovation, leading to higher levels of engagement and productivity.

Mentorship goes beyond traditional hierarchical relationships; it involves guiding, coaching, and sharing experiences to facilitate learning and professional development. Mentors serve as role models, offering insights, advice, and constructive feedback to help individuals navigate challenges and seize opportunities.

Creating a Supportive Culture

Building a supportive culture starts with fostering trust, respect, and psychological safety within the team. When team members feel valued and respected, they are more likely to seek assistance when needed and take risks without fear of judgment or reprisal.

Leaders can cultivate a supportive culture by:

1. Leading by Example: Leaders should model supportive behaviors by actively listening to team members, offering assistance, and demonstrating empathy and understanding.

2. Encouraging Open Communication: Establishing open channels of communication encourages team members to voice their concerns, share ideas, and seek help when facing challenges.

3. Providing Resources: Ensure that team members have access to the resources, tools, and training needed to excel in their roles. This may include technical training, professional development opportunities, or access to support networks.

4. Recognizing and Celebrating Achievements: Acknowledge and celebrate the accomplishments of individual team members to boost morale and reinforce positive behavior.

The Role of Mentorship

Mentorship plays a pivotal role in fostering professional growth and skill development within high-performance teams. Effective mentors offer guidance, support, and constructive feedback to help mentees navigate their career paths and overcome obstacles. Mentorship relationships can take various forms, including formal programs, peer mentoring, or informal coaching arrangements.

Key aspects of effective mentorship include:

1. Setting Clear Expectations: Establish clear goals and expectations for the mentorship relationship to ensure alignment and accountability.

2. Building Trust and Rapport: Foster trust and rapport between mentors and mentees by establishing open communication, confidentiality, and mutual respect.

3. Providing Guidance and Feedback: Offer constructive feedback, guidance, and advice tailored to the individual needs and goals of the mentee.

4. Encouraging Reflection and Growth: Encourage mentees to reflect on their experiences, identify areas for improvement, and set goals for personal and professional development.

5. Facilitating Networking and Opportunities: Help mentees expand their professional networks, connect with relevant stakeholders, and seize opportunities for growth and advancement.

Strategies for Effective Support and Mentorship

To effectively support and mentor team members, leaders can employ various strategies tailored to the needs and preferences of individual team members. Some effective strategies include:

1. Regular Check-ins: Schedule regular one-on-one meetings with team members to discuss their progress, challenges, and goals. Use these meetings as opportunities to provide feedback, offer support, and address any concerns.

2. Coaching and Development Plans: Collaborate with team members to create personalized development plans outlining their career aspirations, strengths, areas for improvement, and actionable steps for growth.

3. Skill-Building Workshops and Training: Organize workshops, training sessions, or skill-building activities to help team members enhance their competencies and stay abreast of industry trends and best practices.

4. Peer Learning and Collaboration: Encourage peer learning and collaboration by facilitating knowledge-sharing sessions, cross-functional projects, or mentorship circles where team members can learn from one another's experiences and expertise.

5. 360-Degree Feedback: Implement a 360-degree feedback mechanism where team members receive input and perspectives from peers, subordinates, and supervisors to gain a holistic view of their performance and areas for development.

6. Recognition and Rewards: Recognize and reward team members for their contributions, achievements, and growth milestones to reinforce positive behavior and motivate continued excellence.

Conclusion

Supporting and mentoring team members is essential for fostering a culture of growth, collaboration, and high performance within organizations. By providing the necessary guidance, resources, and developmental opportunities, leaders can empower individuals to reach their full potential and contribute effectively to the team's success. Investing in support and mentorship not only benefits individual team members but also strengthens the overall resilience, agility, and competitiveness of the organization in today's dynamic and rapidly evolving business landscape.

9. Managing Team Performance and Feedback

9.1 Setting Clear Performance Expectations

Setting clear performance expectations is a cornerstone of effective team management. When team members understand what is expected of them, they are better equipped to align their efforts with organizational goals and deliver results. However, establishing these expectations requires careful consideration and communication. In this section, we will explore the importance of setting clear performance expectations and provide practical strategies for managers to do so effectively.

The Importance of Clear Performance Expectations

Clear performance expectations serve as a roadmap for both managers and team members. They provide clarity on roles, responsibilities, goals, and standards of performance. Without clear expectations, team members may feel uncertain about what is required of them, leading to confusion, frustration, and a lack of direction.

Additionally, clear expectations promote accountability and transparency within the team. When everyone understands what is expected, it becomes easier to hold individuals accountable for their performance and results. This, in turn, fosters a culture of trust and mutual respect, where team members feel empowered to take ownership of their work.

Furthermore, setting clear expectations is essential for driving performance and achieving organizational objectives. When team members have a clear understanding of their goals and how their work contributes to the broader mission, they are more motivated and engaged. This alignment between individual and organizational goals is critical for driving productivity, innovation, and success.

Strategies for Setting Clear Performance Expectations

1. Define Goals and Objectives: Begin by clearly defining the goals and objectives that the team needs to accomplish. These goals should be specific, measurable, achievable, relevant, and time-bound (SMART). Communicate these goals to the team, emphasizing the importance of each objective and how it contributes to the overall success of the organization.

2. Clarify Roles and Responsibilities: Clearly define the roles and responsibilities of each team member to ensure that everyone understands their individual contributions to the team's success. This includes outlining tasks, decision-making authority, and expectations for collaboration and communication. By clarifying roles, you minimize confusion and duplication of effort within the team.

3. Establish Performance Metrics: Identify key performance indicators (KPIs) or metrics that will be used to evaluate individual and team performance. These metrics should be aligned with the team's goals and objectives and provide measurable criteria for success. Regularly communicate these metrics to the team and track progress towards achieving them.

4. Provide Resources and Support: Ensure that team members have the resources, tools, and support they need to succeed in their roles. This may include access to training and development opportunities, technology platforms, and adequate staffing levels. By providing the necessary support, you empower team members to perform at their best and overcome any challenges they may encounter.

5. Set Clear Expectations for Behavior and Conduct: In addition to performance goals, it is essential to set clear expectations for behavior and conduct within the team. This includes communication norms, professionalism, and adherence to organizational values and policies. Clearly outline expectations for how team members should interact with one another and with external stakeholders.

6. Encourage Two-Way Communication: Foster open and transparent communication within the team, where team members feel comfortable expressing their ideas, concerns, and feedback. Encourage regular check-ins between managers and team members to discuss progress, address any issues or challenges, and provide ongoing feedback.

7. Monitor and Adjust Expectations as Needed: Regularly monitor team performance and be prepared to adjust expectations as necessary based on changing priorities, resources, or circumstances. Keep lines of communication open with team members and be responsive to their feedback and input. Flexibility and adaptability are key to maintaining clarity and alignment within the team.

Conclusion

Setting clear performance expectations is essential for leading high-performance teams. By defining goals, clarifying roles, establishing performance metrics, providing support, and fostering open communication, managers can create a shared understanding of what success looks like and empower team members to achieve their full potential. By investing time and effort into setting clear expectations, managers lay the foundation for a cohesive and productive team that is aligned with organizational goals and poised for success.

9.2 Providing Constructive Feedback and Recognition

Providing constructive feedback and recognition is a cornerstone of effective team management. It not only fosters a culture of continuous improvement but also boosts morale and engagement within the team. In this section, we will delve into the strategies and best practices for offering feedback and recognition that inspires growth and development among team members.

The Importance of Constructive Feedback

Feedback is a powerful tool for personal and professional growth. When delivered effectively, it helps individuals understand their strengths and areas for improvement, leading to enhanced performance and productivity. However, delivering feedback can be challenging, as it requires a delicate balance between honesty and tact.

Key Principles of Constructive Feedback:

1. Timeliness: Feedback should be provided promptly, ideally soon after the observed behavior or performance.

2. Specificity: Vague feedback is not actionable. Be specific about the behaviors or actions that you are addressing.

3. Focus on Behavior: Feedback should focus on observable behaviors rather than personal characteristics.

4. Balanced Approach: Highlight both strengths and areas for improvement to provide a balanced perspective.

5. Two-Way Communication: Encourage dialogue and active listening to ensure that feedback is well-received and understood.

Strategies for Providing Constructive Feedback

1. Prepare in Advance:

Before delivering feedback, take the time to gather relevant information and examples to support your observations. Consider the impact of the feedback and how it aligns with the individual's goals and objectives.

2. Choose the Right Time and Place:

Select a suitable environment for delivering feedback, ensuring privacy and minimizing distractions. Timing is crucial; choose a moment when the recipient is receptive and available to engage in a constructive conversation.

3. Use the Situation-Behavior-Impact (SBI) Model:

The SBI model provides a structured framework for delivering feedback:

   - *Situation:* Describe the specific context or situation in which the behavior occurred.

   - *Behavior:* Outline the observable behavior or action that you are addressing.

   - *Impact:* Explain the impact of the behavior on the team, project, or organization, focusing on outcomes or consequences.

4. Focus on Improvement:

Frame feedback as an opportunity for growth and development rather than criticism. Emphasize how addressing the identified areas for improvement can contribute to the individual's success and the team's overall performance.

5. Encourage Self-Reflection:

Encourage recipients to reflect on their performance and identify strategies for improvement independently. Offer support and guidance in setting actionable goals and implementing changes.

Recognition and Appreciation

In addition to providing constructive feedback, recognizing and appreciating team members' contributions is vital for maintaining morale and motivation. Recognition can take various forms, from informal gestures of appreciation to formal awards and incentives.

Principles of Effective Recognition:

1. Frequent and Timely: Recognize achievements promptly to reinforce desired behaviors and outcomes.

2. Personalized: Tailor recognition to individual preferences and preferences, acknowledging unique contributions and strengths.

3. Public and Private: While public recognition boosts morale and reinforces positive behaviors, some individuals may prefer private acknowledgment.

4. Sincere and Specific: Genuine appreciation resonates with recipients. Be specific about what you are recognizing and why it matters.

5. Aligned with Values and Goals: Ensure that recognition aligns with organizational values and goals, reinforcing desired behaviors and outcomes.

Strategies for Effective Recognition:

1. Verbal Praise: Express appreciation through verbal recognition, highlighting specific accomplishments and contributions.

2. Written Notes or Emails: A handwritten note or personalized email can have a lasting impact, conveying sincerity and appreciation.

3. Public Acknowledgment: Recognize achievements in team meetings, newsletters, or other forums to celebrate success and inspire others.

4. Opportunities for Growth: Provide opportunities for professional development and advancement as a form of recognition for exceptional performance.

5. Peer-to-Peer Recognition: Encourage a culture of peer recognition, where team members acknowledge and appreciate each other's efforts.

Conclusion

Effective feedback and recognition are essential components of a high-performance team culture. By providing constructive feedback, managers empower individuals to reach their full potential and contribute to the team's success. Similarly, recognition and appreciation reinforce positive behaviors and foster a sense of belonging and commitment within the team. By adopting strategies that prioritize open communication, empathy, and continuous improvement, managers can cultivate a supportive and collaborative work environment where every team member feels valued and motivated to excel.

Example Illustrating Constructive Feedback:

Scenario: Emily is a project manager responsible for overseeing a team of developers working on a critical software project. During a sprint review meeting, Emily noticed that one of her team members, Alex, consistently missed the deadlines for delivering his tasks, causing delays in the project timeline.

Constructive Feedback Session:

Emily: "Alex, I'd like to discuss your recent performance during our sprint reviews. In the last few iterations, we've observed that some of your tasks were not completed by the agreed-upon deadlines. For example, during the last sprint, your task to implement the user authentication feature was delayed by two days."

Situation: "During our sprint reviews..."

Behavior: "...some of your tasks were not completed by the agreed-upon deadlines. For example, during the last sprint, your task to implement the user authentication feature was delayed by two days."

Impact: "These delays have had a significant impact on our project timeline, causing delays in subsequent tasks and jeopardizing our overall delivery schedule. It's essential for our team to meet our commitments to ensure the success of the project."

Emily: "I understand that unexpected challenges may arise during the development process, but it's crucial to communicate any issues or roadblocks as soon as possible so that we can adjust our plans accordingly. Can you share any insights into what may have contributed to these delays?"

Open Dialogue: Emily encourages Alex to share any challenges he may be facing, fostering open communication and collaboration to address performance issues effectively.

Example Illustrating Recognition and Appreciation:

Scenario: After successfully completing a challenging project milestone, Emily wants to recognize and appreciate the efforts of her team members.

Recognition and Appreciation Session:

Emily: "Team, I want to take a moment to recognize the outstanding effort and dedication that each of you has demonstrated throughout this project. Despite facing numerous challenges and tight deadlines, we have successfully delivered the latest milestone on time and with exceptional quality."

Public Acknowledgment: Emily publicly acknowledges the team's achievements during a team meeting, highlighting their collective efforts and contributions.

Emily: "I'd like to give a special shout-out to Sarah for her exceptional problem-solving skills during the testing phase, which ensured that we identified and resolved critical issues before the deadline. Your attention to detail and commitment to quality are truly commendable, Sarah."

Sincere and Specific Recognition: Emily provides specific praise to Sarah, acknowledging her unique contributions and strengths.

Emily: "I also want to thank the entire team for their collaboration, resilience, and unwavering dedication to our project goals. Each one of you plays a vital role in our success, and I'm grateful to have such a talented and committed team."

Frequent and Timely Recognition: By recognizing the team's achievements promptly and sincerely, Emily reinforces positive behaviors and fosters a culture of appreciation within the team.

Example Illustrating Recognition and Appreciation (continued):

Scenario: As the project progresses, Emily continues to reinforce a culture of recognition and appreciation among her team members.

Recognition and Appreciation in Action:

Emily: "Team, as we wrap up another successful sprint, I want to take a moment to acknowledge the outstanding contributions of our team members. Each of you has played a crucial role in delivering high-quality work and meeting our project objectives."

Frequent and Timely Recognition: Emily ensures that recognition is a regular part of team interactions, reinforcing positive behaviors and outcomes.

Emily: "I'd like to highlight the collaboration between Jack and Lisa during the development of the new feature. Their teamwork and coordination significantly streamlined the implementation process and resulted in a more efficient solution."

Peer-to-Peer Recognition: By recognizing the collaboration between Jack and Lisa, Emily encourages a culture of peer acknowledgment, where team members appreciate each other's efforts and contributions.

Emily: "Additionally, I want to express my appreciation to Tom for his proactive approach to problem-solving. His quick response to an unexpected issue prevented a potential delay and kept our project on track."

Personalized Recognition: Emily tailors recognition to individual contributions, acknowledging unique strengths and efforts.

Emily: "Finally, I want to thank each of you for your dedication and commitment to our team's success. Your hard work and professionalism are truly commendable, and I look forward to achieving even greater milestones together in the future."

Conclusion:

In this example, Emily demonstrates effective leadership by actively recognizing and appreciating the contributions of her team members. By providing frequent and timely recognition, acknowledging specific achievements, and fostering a culture of appreciation, Emily cultivates a positive work environment where team members feel valued, motivated, and engaged. This, in turn, enhances morale, productivity, and collaboration, ultimately contributing to the team's success and the achievement of organizational goals.

9.3 Addressing Performance Issues Effectively

Addressing performance issues within a team is a critical aspect of maintaining its efficiency and ensuring the achievement of organizational goals. When left unattended, even minor performance issues can escalate, affecting team morale, productivity, and ultimately, the bottom line. However, effectively addressing these issues requires a delicate balance of empathy, clear communication, and proactive problem-solving. In this section, we will explore strategies and best practices for identifying, addressing, and resolving performance issues within a team.

1. Identifying Performance Issues

Before performance issues can be addressed, they must first be identified. This requires ongoing monitoring and evaluation of individual and team performance. Some common signs that may indicate performance issues include:

- Decreased productivity or quality of work
- Missed deadlines or frequent errors
- Lack of engagement or motivation
- Negative attitude or behavior towards colleagues
- Increased absenteeism or tardiness
- Failure to meet established goals or objectives

Managers and team leaders should remain vigilant for these indicators and be proactive in addressing them before they escalate.

2. Understanding the Root Causes

Once performance issues have been identified, it is essential to understand their underlying causes. Performance issues can stem from a variety of factors, including:

- Lack of skills or training

- Poor fit between the individual and their role

- Personal problems or external stressors

- Inadequate resources or support

- Misalignment of goals or expectations

- Communication barriers or conflicts within the team

By identifying the root causes of performance issues, managers can develop targeted strategies to address them effectively.

3. Providing Constructive Feedback

Effective feedback is essential for addressing performance issues in a constructive manner. When providing feedback to team members, managers should:

- Be specific and objective: Clearly articulate the behaviors or outcomes that need improvement, providing concrete examples where possible.
- Focus on the issue, not the individual: Avoid personal attacks and instead focus on addressing the performance issue itself.
- Offer support and guidance: Provide resources, training, or mentoring to help the individual improve their performance.
- Encourage open communication: Create a safe and supportive environment where team members feel comfortable discussing their challenges and seeking assistance.

4. Setting Clear Expectations

Clear expectations are crucial for preventing and addressing performance issues. Managers should ensure that team members understand their roles, responsibilities, and performance goals from the outset. This may involve:

- Clearly defining job roles and responsibilities

- Establishing measurable performance objectives and benchmarks

- Communicating expectations regarding quality standards, deadlines, and accountability

- Providing regular updates and feedback on performance against established goals

When team members know what is expected of them, they are better equipped to meet those expectations and address any performance issues that may arise.

5. Offering Support and Resources

In some cases, performance issues may be due to factors beyond the individual's control, such as a lack of resources or support. Managers should proactively identify any obstacles or challenges that may be hindering performance and take steps to address them. This may involve:

- Providing additional training or development opportunities

- Allocating more time or resources to complete tasks

- Adjusting workloads or priorities to reduce overwhelm

- Offering coaching or mentoring to help individuals overcome specific challenges

- Facilitating collaboration and teamwork to leverage collective strengths and expertise

By offering the necessary support and resources, managers can empower team members to overcome obstacles and improve their performance.

6. Addressing Underlying Issues

In some cases, performance issues may be symptomatic of deeper underlying issues within the team or organization. These may include:

- Communication breakdowns or conflicts within the team
- Lack of clarity or alignment regarding goals and priorities
- Ineffective leadership or management practices
- Organizational culture or systemic issues that undermine performance

To address these underlying issues, managers may need to:

- Facilitate open and honest communication within the team
- Clarify goals, roles, and expectations to ensure alignment
- Address any systemic issues or cultural barriers that may be impeding performance
- Provide leadership training or coaching to enhance managerial effectiveness
- Foster a culture of continuous improvement and learning within the organization

By addressing these underlying issues, managers can create an environment that fosters high performance and supports the ongoing success of the team.

7. Implementing Performance Improvement Plans

In cases where performance issues persist despite efforts to address them, managers may need to implement formal performance improvement plans (PIPs). A PIP is a structured approach to addressing performance issues that typically includes:

- Clearly defined performance goals and expectations

- A timeline for improvement, with specific milestones and deadlines

- Regular monitoring and feedback to track progress

- Consequences for failing to meet agreed-upon targets

- Support and resources to help the individual improve their performance

PIPs should be developed in collaboration with the individual and clearly communicated to ensure mutual understanding and accountability.

8. Knowing When to Seek Outside Assistance

In some situations, addressing performance issues may require outside assistance or intervention. This could involve:

- Consulting with HR professionals or organizational development experts for guidance

- Seeking mediation or conflict resolution services to address interpersonal conflicts

- Providing access to employee assistance programs or counseling services for individuals experiencing personal or emotional challenges

- Engaging external consultants or specialists to conduct assessments or provide training in specific areas of need

Managers should be willing to seek outside assistance when necessary to ensure that performance issues are addressed effectively and professionally.

Conclusion

Effectively addressing performance issues within a team requires a proactive and multi-faceted approach. By identifying performance issues early, understanding their root causes, and providing constructive feedback and support, managers can help individuals overcome challenges and improve their performance. Clear communication, setting clear expectations, and addressing underlying issues are essential components of this process. By implementing performance improvement plans and knowing when to seek outside assistance, managers can create an environment that fosters high performance and supports the ongoing success of the team.

10. Navigating Challenges and Overcoming Obstacles

10.1 Identifying Common Team Challenges

In the dynamic landscape of team dynamics, challenges are an inevitable aspect of the journey towards high performance. Identifying these challenges is the first step towards addressing them effectively. Let's delve into some of the most common obstacles teams encounter:

Communication Breakdowns

Effective communication is the lifeblood of any successful team. However, breakdowns in communication can impede progress and breed misunderstandings. These breakdowns may manifest as unclear instructions, misinterpretations of messages, or simply a lack of communication channels altogether. When team members are not on the same page, it can lead to inefficiencies, frustration, and ultimately, diminished performance.

Conflict and Disagreements

Differences in opinions, work styles, and personalities are inevitable when individuals come together to collaborate. While some level of conflict can be healthy, unresolved disputes can escalate and disrupt team cohesion. Whether it's conflicting priorities, interpersonal tensions, or disagreements over approaches, managing and resolving conflicts is essential for maintaining a harmonious and productive team environment.

Lack of Clarity and Direction

Ambiguity breeds confusion and uncertainty within teams. When team members are unsure about their roles, responsibilities, or the overall objectives of their work, it can hinder progress and demotivate individuals. Lack of clarity may stem from vague goals, undefined processes, or inadequate guidance from leadership. Without a clear sense of direction, teams may struggle to stay focused and aligned towards common goals.

Poor Decision-Making

Effective decision-making is crucial for driving progress and achieving results. However, teams may encounter challenges related to decision-making processes, such as indecisiveness, consensus-seeking, or decision paralysis. Additionally, biases, groupthink, and power dynamics within the team can also impede the quality of decisions made. Overcoming these obstacles requires fostering a culture of transparency, open dialogue, and critical thinking within the team.

Resource Constraints

Limited resources, whether it's budgetary constraints, time limitations, or inadequate access to tools and technology, can pose significant challenges for teams. When resources are scarce, teams may struggle to meet deadlines, deliver quality work, or innovate effectively. It requires creative problem-solving and efficient resource allocation to overcome these constraints and maximize the team's productivity and impact.

Lack of Trust and Psychological Safety

Trust is the foundation of any high-performing team. Without trust, individuals may hesitate to take risks, share ideas, or collaborate openly with their team members. Similarly, psychological safety, which encompasses the ability to express oneself without fear of reprisal or judgment, is essential for fostering innovation and creativity within teams. Building and maintaining trust and psychological safety requires consistent effort and commitment from both leaders and team members.

External Distractions and Pressures

External factors, such as market volatility, industry disruptions, or changes in organizational priorities, can exert pressure on teams and divert their attention from their goals. Additionally, individual team members may face personal challenges or external obligations that impact their focus and availability. Managing these external distractions and pressures requires adaptability, resilience, and effective prioritization strategies.

Cultural and Diversity Challenges

In today's globalized world, teams often comprise individuals from diverse cultural backgrounds, experiences, and perspectives. While diversity can enrich team dynamics and drive innovation, it can also present challenges related to communication, collaboration, and conflict resolution. Cultural differences in communication styles, decision-making processes, and work norms may require proactive efforts to bridge gaps and foster inclusivity within the team.

Technology Limitations and Dependencies

In an increasingly digital workplace, reliance on technology is pervasive. However, technological dependencies and limitations can hinder team performance if systems fail, tools malfunction, or team members lack the necessary digital literacy skills. Moreover, remote or distributed teams may face additional challenges related to connectivity, accessibility, and cybersecurity. Overcoming these obstacles requires investing in robust technology infrastructure, providing training and support, and fostering a culture of digital fluency within the team.

Conclusion

While these challenges may seem daunting, they are not insurmountable. By recognizing and understanding the common obstacles that teams face, leaders can proactively implement strategies to address them and foster a culture of resilience, collaboration, and continuous improvement within their teams. In the following sections, we will explore strategies and best practices for overcoming these challenges and navigating the path towards sustained high performance.

10.2 Implementing Strategies for Overcoming Obstacles

Successfully navigating challenges and overcoming obstacles is integral to the sustained high performance of any team. While challenges may vary depending on the nature of the team, its goals, and the external environment, there are several universal strategies that managers can employ to empower their teams to overcome obstacles effectively. In this section, we will delve into these strategies and explore how they can be implemented within your team.

1. Foster Open Communication and Transparency

Effective communication lies at the heart of overcoming obstacles within a team. Encouraging open dialogue ensures that team members feel comfortable expressing concerns, sharing ideas, and seeking help when needed. As a manager, it's essential to foster an environment where transparency is valued, and communication channels are accessible to all.

Key Actions:

- Hold regular team meetings where members can discuss challenges openly.

- Encourage team members to voice their opinions and perspectives without fear of judgment.

- Implement communication tools and platforms that facilitate seamless interaction among team members.

- Lead by example by being transparent in your decision-making processes and sharing relevant information with the team.

Benefits:

- Enhances trust and collaboration among team members.

- Promotes a culture of accountability and problem-solving.

- Enables quick identification and resolution of obstacles before they escalate.

Example:

Imagine a software development team facing a critical deadline for a project. During a team meeting, one of the developers expresses concerns about the feasibility of meeting the deadline due to unforeseen technical challenges. Thanks to the open communication culture fostered by the manager, the developer feels comfortable sharing these concerns without fear of retribution. As a result, the team engages in a constructive discussion, brainstorming potential solutions and reallocating resources as necessary to address the challenges proactively. Through transparent communication, the team maintains alignment and confidence in their ability to overcome obstacles together.

2. Empower Problem-Solving Skills

Empowering team members with strong problem-solving skills equips them to tackle obstacles effectively and independently. Encourage a proactive approach to problem-solving by providing resources, training, and support to enhance critical thinking and analytical abilities within your team.

Key Actions:

- Offer training workshops or seminars focused on problem-solving techniques and methodologies.

- Assign challenging tasks or projects that require innovative solutions.

- Establish mentorship programs where experienced team members can guide others in overcoming obstacles.

- Encourage experimentation and risk-taking, emphasizing the importance of learning from failures.

Benefits:

- Builds confidence and self-efficacy among team members.

- Stimulates creativity and innovation in problem-solving approaches.

- Reduces reliance on managerial intervention for every obstacle encountered.

Example:

Consider a marketing team tasked with launching a new product in a highly competitive market. When faced with unexpected changes in consumer preferences, team members leverage their problem-solving skills to adapt their marketing strategies accordingly. The manager provides support by organizing a workshop on market research techniques and encouraging team members to analyze data trends and consumer behavior independently. Empowered with the necessary skills and resources, the team identifies innovative marketing approaches that resonate with the target audience, ultimately leading to a successful product launch despite initial setbacks.

3. Promote Flexibility and Adaptability

In today's dynamic business environment, adaptability is key to overcoming obstacles effectively. Encourage flexibility within your team by promoting a mindset that embraces change and uncertainty. Equip team members with the tools and resources they need to adapt quickly to shifting circumstances.

Key Actions:

- Incorporate agile methodologies into your team's workflow to enable rapid adaptation to changing priorities.

- Provide training on resilience-building techniques to help team members cope with unexpected challenges.

- Foster a culture that celebrates adaptability and rewards individuals who demonstrate flexibility in their approach.

- Encourage cross-functional collaboration to leverage diverse perspectives and skills in problem-solving.

Benefits:

- Enhances the team's ability to respond promptly to unforeseen obstacles.

- Increases overall resilience and capacity to withstand adversity.

- Positions the team for long-term success in a constantly evolving landscape.

Example:

In a customer service team, sudden spikes in customer inquiries due to a product recall challenge the team's ability to maintain service levels. Instead of adhering rigidly to existing protocols, the team embraces flexibility and adaptability to meet the increased demand. The manager encourages team members to collaborate across departments, temporarily reallocating resources from less critical tasks to address customer concerns promptly. By adopting an agile mindset and adjusting workflows as needed, the team demonstrates resilience in the face of adversity, preserving customer satisfaction and brand reputation.

4. Establish Clear Goals and Priorities

Clarity of purpose is essential for guiding teams through obstacles and challenges effectively. Ensure that your team understands its goals, priorities, and expectations, allowing members to align their efforts accordingly. By establishing a clear roadmap, you provide the framework within which obstacles can be addressed with purpose and determination.

Key Actions:

- Clearly communicate the team's objectives, both short-term and long-term, ensuring alignment with broader organizational goals.

- Break down larger goals into smaller, actionable tasks, providing clarity on individual responsibilities.

- Regularly revisit and reassess goals in response to changing circumstances, keeping the team focused on the most pressing priorities.

- Foster a sense of ownership and accountability among team members for achieving collective goals.

Benefits:

- Minimizes confusion and ambiguity, enabling the team to stay on course despite obstacles.

- Enhances motivation and commitment by providing a clear sense of purpose.

- Facilitates efficient allocation of resources towards achieving strategic objectives.

Example:

A project management team embarks on a complex infrastructure upgrade project for a large corporation. To ensure clarity and alignment, the manager establishes clear goals and priorities at the outset, outlining key milestones and deliverables. Regular progress reviews and goal reassessments enable the team to stay on track despite encountering unforeseen logistical challenges and resource constraints. By maintaining focus on the overarching objectives, the team successfully navigates obstacles, delivering the project on time and within budget, much to the satisfaction of the client.

5. Cultivate a Supportive Team Culture

A supportive team culture is a powerful asset in overcoming obstacles, as it fosters camaraderie, trust, and mutual assistance among team members. Invest in building strong relationships within your team, creating a supportive ecosystem where individuals feel valued, respected, and empowered to overcome challenges together.

Key Actions:

- Encourage teamwork and collaboration through team-building activities and exercises.

- Recognize and celebrate individual and collective achievements, reinforcing a sense of camaraderie and shared success.

- Foster a culture of empathy and understanding, where team members are encouraged to offer support and assistance to one another.

- Address conflicts and issues promptly, promoting a respectful and inclusive work environment.

Benefits:

- Strengthens team cohesion and solidarity, enabling members to rally together in the face of adversity.

- Enhances morale and job satisfaction, leading to increased productivity and performance.

- Creates a sense of belonging and loyalty, reducing turnover and fostering long-term commitment.

Example:

In a sales team, individual representatives face rejection and setbacks on a daily basis while pursuing ambitious sales targets. Recognizing the importance of morale and camaraderie, the manager cultivates a supportive team culture where wins and losses are celebrated collectively. Team members regularly share success stories and offer encouragement during challenging periods, fostering a sense of belonging and mutual support. As a result, even during tough times, team morale remains high, motivating individuals to persevere and collaborate towards achieving shared goals.

6. Leverage Technology and Automation

Technology can be a valuable ally in overcoming obstacles by streamlining processes, improving efficiency, and providing valuable insights for decision-making. Explore technological solutions and automation tools that can help your team overcome common obstacles more effectively, freeing up time and resources for strategic initiatives.

Key Actions:

- Invest in project management software that enables real-time collaboration, task tracking, and resource allocation.

- Implement data analytics tools to gather insights and identify patterns that can inform problem-solving strategies.

- Explore automation opportunities to streamline repetitive tasks and reduce the likelihood of human error.

- Stay informed about emerging technologies and trends relevant to your industry, remaining agile and adaptable in your approach.

Benefits:

- Increases efficiency and productivity by eliminating manual inefficiencies and bottlenecks.

- Provides valuable data-driven insights for informed decision-making and problem-solving.

- Enables scalability and flexibility to accommodate evolving business needs and challenges.

Example:

An HR team responsible for processing employee benefits experiences a surge in paperwork due to a company-wide restructuring. To streamline operations and reduce manual workload, the manager implements an automated HR management system. The new system digitizes document processing, streamlines approval workflows, and generates reports automatically, significantly reducing administrative burden and minimizing errors. With more time freed up for strategic initiatives, the HR team can focus on providing enhanced support to employees during the transition period, ensuring a smooth and efficient process for all stakeholders involved.

Conclusion

Overcoming obstacles is an inevitable part of any team's journey towards high performance. By implementing these strategies and fostering a supportive environment conducive to innovation and collaboration, managers can empower their teams to navigate challenges with resilience, agility, and determination. Remember, obstacles are not roadblocks but opportunities for growth and learning, and with the right mindset and approach, they can propel your team towards greater success.

10.3 Building Resilience and Adaptability in Your Team

In the dynamic landscape of modern business, resilience and adaptability are no longer just desirable traits; they are indispensable qualities for high-performance teams. As a manager, fostering resilience and adaptability within your team can be a game-changer, enabling them to weather storms, pivot effectively, and thrive in the face of adversity. This section delves into strategies for cultivating these crucial attributes within your team.

Understanding Resilience and Adaptability

Before delving into strategies for building resilience and adaptability, it's essential to understand what these terms entail.

Resilience refers to the ability to bounce back from setbacks, challenges, or failures. It involves not just surviving adversity but emerging stronger and more capable as a result.

Adaptability encompasses the capacity to adjust to new conditions, environments, or demands. It involves being flexible, open-minded, and resourceful in the face of change.

Together, resilience and adaptability form a powerful combination that enables teams to navigate uncertainties and capitalize on opportunities effectively.

Cultivating Resilience

1. Promote a Growth Mindset: Encourage team members to adopt a growth mindset, emphasizing that setbacks are opportunities for learning and growth rather than failures. Foster a culture where mistakes are viewed as valuable learning experiences rather than reasons for blame.

2. Provide Support and Encouragement: Be proactive in offering support and encouragement to team members facing challenges. Create an environment where team members feel safe to express their concerns and seek assistance when needed.

3. Celebrate Small Wins: Recognize and celebrate the achievements and progress, no matter how small. Celebrating even minor victories boosts morale, fosters a sense of accomplishment, and reinforces resilience.

4. Encourage Self-Care: Emphasize the importance of self-care and work-life balance. Encourage team members to prioritize their well-being by taking breaks, practicing mindfulness, and engaging in activities that recharge them mentally and emotionally.

5. Lead by Example: Demonstrate resilience in your own actions and responses to challenges. Your team looks to you for guidance, so modeling resilience sets a powerful example and encourages them to follow suit.

Example 1: Promote a Growth Mindset

Imagine a project team working on a tight deadline to deliver a crucial product update. Despite meticulous planning, they encounter unexpected technical issues that delay progress. Instead of assigning blame or becoming discouraged, the team leader gathers everyone for a quick huddle. They frame the setback as an opportunity to learn, highlighting what went well and identifying areas for improvement. Team members are encouraged to brainstorm solutions collaboratively, fostering a sense of ownership and resilience in the face of adversity.

Example 2: Provide Support and Encouragement

During a challenging period of organizational restructuring, a marketing team finds themselves grappling with increased workloads and uncertainty about the future. The team manager holds individual meetings with each team member to check in on their well-being and discuss any concerns they may have. They offer emotional support, reassurance, and practical assistance where needed, helping team members feel valued and supported during a turbulent time.

Fostering Adaptability

1. Encourage Continuous Learning: Create opportunities for team members to expand their skills and knowledge continuously. Encourage participation in training programs, workshops, and seminars to stay updated with industry trends and developments.

2. Embrace Change: Cultivate a culture where change is embraced rather than feared. Help team members understand that change brings opportunities for growth and innovation, and equip them with the tools and mindset to adapt effectively.

3. Encourage Innovation and Creativity: Foster an environment where new ideas are welcomed and experimentation is encouraged. Encourage team members to think outside the box, explore alternative solutions, and take calculated risks.

4. Facilitate Open Communication: Establish channels for open and transparent communication within the team. Encourage dialogue, feedback, and collaboration to foster a culture of adaptability where ideas can be freely exchanged, and solutions co-created.

5. Provide Resources and Support: Ensure that your team has access to the resources, training, and support needed to adapt to new challenges effectively. Whether it's providing access to technology, offering mentorship, or facilitating cross-functional collaboration, invest in your team's ability to navigate change.

<u>Example 3: Embrace Change</u>

In a rapidly evolving industry, a software development team recognizes the need to adapt their processes to stay competitive. Rather than clinging to outdated methods, they embrace change enthusiastically. The team leader introduces agile principles, encouraging shorter development cycles, frequent feedback loops, and greater collaboration between developers and stakeholders. Initially met with skepticism, the new approach soon proves its effectiveness as the team becomes more responsive to customer needs and delivers higher-quality products.

<u>Example 4: Encourage Innovation and Creativity</u>

Facing stiff competition in the market, a product design team decides to take a bold approach by encouraging innovation and creativity in their projects. They set aside time for brainstorming sessions and idea generation, inviting team members from different disciplines to contribute their perspectives. Through experimentation and prototyping, the team develops innovative features and solutions that set their products apart from competitors, driving growth and customer satisfaction.

Integrating Resilience and Adaptability into Team Practices

1. Regular Check-Ins: Schedule regular check-ins with team members to assess their well-being, workload, and any challenges they may be facing. Use these meetings as opportunities to provide support, guidance, and resources as needed.

2. *Scenario Planning:* Conduct scenario planning exercises to prepare your team for potential challenges and disruptions. Encourage them to brainstorm alternative courses of action and develop contingency plans to mitigate risks proactively.

3. *Promote Collaboration and Cross-Training*: Encourage collaboration and cross-training among team members to build a diverse skill set and enhance adaptability. By sharing knowledge and expertise, team members become more versatile and better equipped to handle a variety of tasks and responsibilities.

4. *Encourage Feedback and Reflection:* Create a culture of continuous improvement by soliciting feedback from team members and encouraging self-reflection. Regularly evaluate team processes, identify areas for improvement, and implement changes to enhance resilience and adaptability.

5. *Lead with Empathy:* Finally, lead with empathy and compassion. Recognize that each team member may respond to challenges differently and tailor your approach accordingly. Show understanding, provide support, and foster a sense of belonging within the team.

Example 5: Regular Check-Ins

A remote customer support team, scattered across different time zones, faces unique challenges in maintaining cohesion and morale. The team leader implements regular virtual check-ins using video conferencing tools. These check-ins provide an opportunity for team members to share updates, discuss challenges, and offer support to one another. By fostering open communication and connection, the team feels more resilient and cohesive despite the distance.

Example 6: Promote Collaboration and Cross-Training

In a cross-functional project team, team members are encouraged to step outside their comfort zones and learn new skills. Developers attend design workshops, marketers learn about coding basics, and project managers shadow each other to gain insights into different aspects of the project lifecycle. This cross-training not only enhances individual adaptability but also fosters a culture of collaboration and mutual support within the team.

Conclusion

Building resilience and adaptability within your team is an ongoing process that requires commitment, patience, and effort. By fostering a growth mindset, providing support, encouraging innovation, and leading by example, you can empower your team to thrive in the face of adversity and uncertainty. Remember that resilience and adaptability are not just individual traits but collective strengths that contribute to the overall success and performance of your team. Invest in cultivating these qualities, and watch as your team rises to meet challenges with confidence and resilience.

Conclusion

In conclusion, building high-performance teams is both an art and a science. It requires a blend of leadership skills, emotional intelligence, strategic planning, and continuous learning. Throughout this guide, we have explored various aspects of team building, from forming the right team composition to fostering a culture of collaboration and accountability. As managers, our role is not just to oversee the work of our teams but to empower them to reach their full potential.

One of the key takeaways from this guide is the importance of communication in team dynamics. Effective communication serves as the foundation for building trust, resolving conflicts, and aligning team goals with organizational objectives. By fostering open and transparent communication channels, managers can create an environment where team members feel valued and heard.

Another critical aspect of building high-performance teams is creating a culture of psychological safety. When team members feel safe to express their ideas, voice concerns, and take calculated risks, they are more likely to innovate and collaborate effectively. As managers, it is our responsibility to cultivate this culture by encouraging constructive feedback, celebrating successes, and embracing failure as a learning opportunity.

Additionally, diversity and inclusion play a crucial role in team effectiveness. By embracing diverse perspectives, backgrounds, and experiences, teams can tackle complex problems from multiple angles and drive innovation. Managers should actively seek to build diverse teams and create an inclusive environment where every member feels respected and valued.

CONCLUSION

Furthermore, empowering team members to take ownership of their work is essential for fostering a sense of ownership and accountability. By setting clear goals, providing autonomy, and offering support when needed, managers can enable their teams to perform at their best. Empowered teams are more motivated, engaged, and committed to achieving shared objectives.

Continuous learning and development are also vital for maintaining high team performance. As the business landscape evolves, teams must adapt and acquire new skills to stay competitive. Managers should invest in training programs, mentorship opportunities, and knowledge sharing initiatives to keep their teams ahead of the curve.

Lastly, it's essential for managers to lead by example and embody the values and behaviors they expect from their teams. By demonstrating integrity, resilience, and a growth mindset, managers can inspire their teams to overcome challenges and strive for excellence. Leadership is not just about directing; it's about inspiring and empowering others to become the best versions of themselves.

In closing, building high-performance teams requires dedication, patience, and a commitment to continuous improvement. By focusing on communication, psychological safety, diversity, empowerment, learning, and leadership, managers can create a team culture that thrives in today's dynamic business environment. Remember, the journey to building a high-performance team is ongoing, but the rewards of success are immeasurable. Together, let's continue to empower our teams and unlock their full potential.

CONCLUSION

Thank you

As we reflect on the journey of bringing this book to fruition, we are filled with profound gratitude for the support and encouragement we have received along the way. Building High-Performance Teams has been a labor of love, and we are deeply thankful to each and every one of you who has played a part in making this endeavor possible.

First and foremost, we extend our heartfelt appreciation to our readers. Your interest in enhancing your leadership skills and fostering high-performance teams is what motivates us to continue our work in this field. We hope that the insights, strategies, and practical advice shared within these pages will empower you to navigate the complexities of team dynamics and unlock the full potential of your teams.

We are immensely grateful to our families for their unwavering support throughout the writing process. Your patience, understanding, and encouragement have been instrumental in helping us balance the demands of authorship with our personal lives. To our spouses, children, parents, and extended family members, thank you for being our pillars of strength and source of inspiration.

A project of this magnitude would not have been possible without the expertise and guidance of numerous individuals who generously shared their knowledge and insights. We extend our sincere thanks to our colleagues, mentors, and industry experts who contributed their expertise to enrich the content of this book. Your invaluable input has undoubtedly elevated the quality of our work and expanded its breadth of coverage.

We are indebted to the dedicated professionals who assisted us in various stages of the publication process. From editors and proofreaders to designers and publishers, your meticulous attention to detail and commitment to excellence have played a vital role in shaping the final product. We deeply appreciate your efforts in helping us bring our vision to life.

CONCLUSION

Our heartfelt thanks also go out to the reviewers and endorsers who provided valuable feedback and endorsements for this book. Your endorsement serves as a testament to the relevance and significance of the ideas presented herein, and we are truly grateful for your support.

Last but certainly not least, we would like to express our profound gratitude to the countless individuals who inspire us daily with their dedication to building high-performance teams. Whether you are a frontline manager, a seasoned executive, or an aspiring leader, your commitment to fostering collaboration, driving innovation, and nurturing talent serves as a beacon of hope in an increasingly complex and interconnected world.

In closing, we extend our warmest thanks to each and every one of you who has joined us on this journey. May the insights shared within these pages empower you to lead with clarity, compassion, and conviction, and may your efforts to build high-performance teams pave the way for a brighter future for all.

With sincere appreciation,

www.ingramcontent.com/pod-product-compliance
Lightning Source LLC
Chambersburg PA
CBHW062107220526
45471CB00010B/3633